Sue The Bastards!

YOUR GUIDE TO HUGH CASH AWARDS, LIFETIME PAYMENTS AND MAXIMUM DAMAGES

The facts on how to collect money from corporations, stock-brokers, businessmen, or anyone who has caused you financial injury or loss with special sections on how to recover for personal injuries.

by

James J. Shapiro

DISCLAIMER:

This publication is designed to provide general information about claims for personal and financial injuries. No lawyer should give legal advice about a specific problem or question unless he or she knows all of the facts and circumstances surrounding the case and the client. Buying or reading this book does not make you a client of the author. You become a client by making an agreement for representation with a particular lawyer. Such agreements are generally put in writing, in the form of a retainer statement that the lawyer will ask you to sign.

The laws in every state vary. Each case has different facts and circumstances. The author and publisher specifically disclaim any personal liability, loss, or risk incurred as a consequence of the use, either directly or indirectly, of any information in this book. The author and publisher are not engaged in rendering legal, accounting, insurance, or other professional services by publishing this book. If legal advice or other expert assistance is required, the services of a competent professional person should be sought.

First Edition—1997
ISBN: 1-883527-06-6

QUESTIONS, FREE UPDATES, AND HOW TO REACH THE AUTHOR

If you have questions about this book . . .

If you would like free updates to this book . . .

If you would like to receive a free newsletter . . .

Contact James Shapiro at 1-800-546-7777

CONTENTS

4

SECTION THREE: EXPOSURE TO TOXIC SUBSTANCES OR DANGEROUS PRODUCTS

SECTION FOUR: MEDICAL MALPRACTICE

SECTION FIVE: STOCKBROKER MISCONDUCT

SECTION FOURTEEN: WORKERS' COMPENSATION CLAIMS

SECTION ONE

INTRODUCTION

DEDICATED TO MY FATHER, SIDNEY

My father has always believed in me. He inspired me to follow in his footsteps and attend law school. Together, we formed the law firm of Shapiro and Shapiro. In March of 1986, I suggested that Shapiro & Shapiro advertise on television. Many people thought that I was too eager to develop the law practice and were against my desire to advertise. My father stood by my side. He understood that advertising would reach injured people who might not otherwise have access to a lawyer.

My father has practiced law for more than 50 years. In those 50 years, he has helped thousands of people. All of the lawyers and judges I meet praise his compassionate heart. I am fortunate to have such an amicable and respectable person as a best friend, business partner, and most importantly, as a Father.

SPECIAL DEDICATION

This book is not complete without a mention of a very special attorney, Lori Henkel. As the senior litigator at Shapiro & Shapiro, she has helped hundreds of clients to recover the cash and benefits that they truly deserve from insurance companies, corporations, and other defendants. Lori fights hard for the rights of people who have been injured. She has contributed greatly to this book and to Shapiro & Shapiro.

To Lori—never give up your drive to win, and thank you for your help with this book.

A PERSONAL INTRODUCTION FROM
JAMES J. SHAPIRO, ESQ.

My name is James Shapiro. I have helped thousands of people collect millions of dollars for their legal claims. I am proud to be known as a tough, smart lawyer who gets results.

I only represent victims of injuries—be they personal injuries or injuries of a financial nature. I never represent corporations or insurance companies. I have one goal. That goal is to help victims of personal and financial injuries collect what is fair and right.

For years, I have fought insurance companies, large corporations, and other defendants. I know that this is the only way to protect my clients' legal rights.

This book contains information about how to obtain cash and benefits if you have suffered losses due to bodily injuries, misrepresentations by stockbrokers or agents of business franchises, or discrimination by an employer or other entity.

For readers who need a lawyer, this book will describe how to hire a lawyer on a contingent fee basis—at no cost unless you win. For readers who are close to settling a claim, this book contains important questions to ask your lawyer before you settle.

I believe the greatest thing I can do as an attorney is to help victims of personal and financial injuries obtain what is just and fair.

WHAT THIS BOOK CAN DO FOR YOU

This book will answer many questions that you may have, and will tell you secrets that insurance companies, product manufacturers, stockbrokers, franchisors, and those who engage in discriminatory conduct hope you will never know:

- What to do if you are in an accident

- What to do if you believe that you have been injured due to exposure to toxic substances

- What to do if you have sustained financial losses due to investments or involvement in a franchise

- What to do if you believe that you have been the victim of discrimination

- What is medical malpractice?

- What is insurance company bad faith?

- What are "toxic torts"?

- What constitutes actionable misconduct by a stockbroker?

- How to win money even if:
  —You were at fault for an accident
  —You were aware that you were being exposed to toxic substances
  —You consented to a risky investment
  —You continued to work for an employer who engaged in discriminatory conduct

- Situations in which you should not speak to the insurance company or representatives of the other side

- How to select the best lawyer for your case

- How to determine the value of your case

- How to decide whether to go to court or settle

- Whether a lawyer can give you a cash advance

- A checklist to review before you settle any case

- Telephone numbers to complain about insurance companies, unsafe products and work conditions, unfair business practices, and discriminatory acts.

Insurance companies, product manufacturers, stockbrokers, franchisors, and employers have investigators, expert witnesses, lawyers, and lots of money. Most individuals lack such resources—and the other side knows it. This book contains information that will help you to fight back. With this information, you can collect the cash and benefits to which you are entitled!

GET ALL OF THE FACTS on how to COLLECT MONEY from INSURANCE COMPANIES, CORPORATIONS, LANDLORDS, STOCKBROKERS, DOCTORS, or ANYONE WHO HAS CAUSED YOU INJURY OR LOSS.

SECTION TWO

ACCIDENTS

INTRODUCTION

What does "personal injury" mean?

Examples of personal injuries are cuts, scars, broken bones, burns, head trauma, and paralysis. Only a person, not a piece of property, can sustain a bodily or personal injury.

Personal injuries often occur as a result of accidents. Common types of accidents that result in personal injuries include automobile collisions, incidents where individuals slip and fall, and injuries resulting from the improper design or construction of products.

If you sustain a personal injury as a result of any type of accident, you will probably have doctor bills and other medical expenses associated with your treatment. You might also lose time from work, and therefore suffer a loss of earnings. In addition, you will probably experience pain and suffering as a result of your injury. Finally, in the case of some injuries, you may be left with a permanent disability. When you bring a lawsuit, you are generally seeking to recover for these items.

Things to do after an accident:

1. Attend to your injuries.

   Call an ambulance if anyone involved in the accident has sustained serious injuries.

   Even if you think that your injuries are minor, you should see a doctor after the accident. Injuries that appear minor can sometimes be serious. Only a doctor can properly evaluate your injuries to determine the proper treatment.

A doctor's statement of your injuries is important for your claim. Insurance companies rely on documents. If you do not see a doctor within 24 hours of an accident, the insurance company could doubt the seriousness of your injury.

2. Report the accident.

For a motor vehicle accident, call the police. The responding officer will file a report that includes the date, time, location, witnesses, and a description of how and why the accident happened. You should also notify your own insurance company promptly after the accident.

If the accident happened on someone else's property, immediately notify the owner, landlord, or manager of the accident. Report as much information about the accident as you can, including exact location of the accident, and the names and addresses of all witnesses and parties involved, and obtain a copy of this report.

3. In the presence of witnesses, ask the other person about the accident.

If the other party admits that the accident was their fault, your case could be strengthened. For example, after a motor vehicle accident where the other driver failed to obey a traffic signal, ask "why didn't you stop for the red light?" If the other party admits that they were not paying attention, your chances of winning in court or negotiating a favorable settlement may be improved.

4. Consult with a lawyer.

If you have been injured in an accident, you will probably want to speak with an experienced personal injury lawyer who is backed by resources of a law firm that specializes in injury claims.

Most personal injury lawyers will not charge you a fee to discuss your case. If your case is accepted, there will usually be no legal fee unless the lawyer collects a settlement for you. Personal injury lawyers usually charge a percentage of the settlement. This fee arrangement is called a "contingent fee". The contingent fee allows victims of accidents to hire the lawyer of their choice even if they have little or no income.

If you do not contact a lawyer, you may not learn about your legal rights or the benefits that are available to you. Further, you run the risk of inadvertently making a statement to a representative of the other side that could jeopardize your claim. If you retain a lawyer, he or she will communicate with the other side on your behalf.

5. Tell your doctor and lawyer about all of your injuries.

If one part of your body is badly injured, you may forget to let your doctor know about other injuries that appear less serious. Yet sometimes these "minor" injuries may be more serious in the long run than the injuries that initially seemed the worst. You should tell your doctor about all of your injuries. You cannot recover for injuries that have not been documented by your doctor.

You should also tell your lawyer about all of your injuries. Your lawyer needs to know the full extent of your injuries to help you get the maximum amount for your claim.

Things you should not do after an accident.

1. Do not leave the scene without reporting the accident.

   Do not leave the accident scene without reporting the accident to the police, property owner, landlord, manager or some other person. To recover on your claim, you must be able to prove that the accident actually happened. If you do not report the accident, the insurance company for the other side might argue that the accident never occurred.

   If your motor vehicle or property was involved in the accident, you should report the incident to your own insurance company.

   The information that you provide when reporting the accident should be brief. Provide only the information necessary to describe how, where, and when the accident occurred.

2. Do not give statements, other than to report the accident.

   Do not make any recorded or written statements to anyone, except to report the accident as described above. The person asking for the statement could be working for the other side. Someone who is working for the other side may ask confusing questions about the accident. They may be recording the conversation. If you become confused while answering such questions, you could hurt your case.

3. Do not delay in seeking medical care.

Even if your injuries are minor, you should seek medical attention. In order to recover for your injuries, a doctor must state what injuries were caused by the accident.

4. Do not miss your medical appointments.

Missing doctor visits may create impressions such as (1) your injuries were not serious enough to justify seeing a doctor; (2) you are not making your best effort to get better; or (3) you made your injuries worse by failing to keep medical appointments. Under such circumstances, the adjuster for the other side's insurance company may believe that you do not care about your case. A person who appears not to care about their injuries may be offered less money than someone who follows all medical advice.

5. Do not sign any documents for the other side without consulting your lawyer.

If you sign a release, a settlement agreement, or a check, you will probably end your rights to make further claims against the responsible parties. You can only settle a case one time. You can not go back and ask for more, even if you are still hurt, get worse, or learn new information that strengthens your case. Never sign anything without your lawyer's advice.

6. Do not allow the other side to review your medical records without consulting your lawyer.

A large part of your claim rests on your medical condition. If you give a medical authorization to an insurance company, the insurance company can get your medical records before you ever see them. Sometimes these records contain inaccurate statements or do not include all of your injuries and complaints.

Sometimes your medical records contain information about a condition that is irrelevant to your claim. Such information could be used against you by the other side. Your lawyer should first review all medical records to determine if the other side is entitled to receive them.

7. Do not submit to a medical examination set up by the other side without consulting your lawyer.

Insurance companies spend millions of dollars each year to conduct medical examinations of people who have been injured. These examinations are performed by doctors chosen by the insurance companies. Such examinations often result in a written opinion that is not favorable for the injured person's case. You should therefore go to an examination by a doctor hired by the other side only if your lawyer advises you to attend.

8. Do not admit fault.

Even if you think you are at fault for the accident, do not make such a statement before consulting with your lawyer. If you state that you were at fault, such admission could be used in court against you.

9. Do not offer to pay for any damage caused by the accident.

Never offer to pay for damages to other people, vehicles or property. You probably have insurance. Only your insurance company should offer to pay money to others.

10. Do not withhold any information about the accident from your lawyer.

To give you the best representation, your lawyer needs to know everything about the accident. Never lie to your lawyer. Tell your lawyer everything, even facts that seem unfavorable. Your lawyer needs to know any unfavorable facts about your claim. He or she can minimize these facts while emphasizing those that support your case.

The insurance company will investigate the accident. This investigation will probably disclose any facts that are not favorable to you. If the insurance company knows about these unfavorable facts, but you have failed to mention them to your lawyer, your lawyer will be at a disadvantage. Further, your version of the accident will seem less believable, and you could receive far less money that your case might be worth.

MOTOR VEHICLE ACCIDENTS

Introduction

To recover money for pain, suffering, and permanent injuries that you have sustained as a result of a motor vehicle accident, you must be able to prove that someone other than you was negligent, or careless, and that such negligence caused you to sustain your injuries. If you are unable to prove that someone else's negligence caused your injuries, you may be unable to recover. For example, going through a red light is a negligent act. But unless an accident and injuries occur as result, the driver who ran the light could not be sued for his or her negligence.

There may also be specific requirements about what kind of injuries you must have in order to bring a case arising out of an automobile accident. Such requirements are generally governed by state law. If you have sustained injuries as a result of a motor vehicle accident, you should consult with a lawyer to learn whether your injuries are compensable.

What insurance coverages are available if you are injured in a motor vehicle accident?

1. No-fault coverage

   In most states, no-fault insurance is required on all motor vehicles (although motorcycles are frequently exempt from this requirement). No-fault insurance generally pays for an injured person's medical expenses and lost earnings due to injuries sustained in a motor vehicle accident. These payments are made to the injured person regardless of who was at fault for the accident.

No-fault insurance is separate from the insurance that may be available to compensate you for your pain, suffering and permanent injuries associated with a motor vehicle accident. The coverage that compensates you for these injuries is called liability or bodily injury coverage.

No-fault coverage is generally paid by the insurance company for the vehicle that you were in when the accident occurred. If you were a pedestrian or on a bicycle, the insurance company for the vehicle that struck you will probably pay for your no-fault benefits.

2. Bodily injury coverage

If you are injured in a motor vehicle accident that was caused by the negligence of someone other than yourself, you may be able to make a claim to recover for your pain, suffering and permanent injuries associated with the accident. The coverage that compensates you for these injuries is called liability or bodily injury coverage. This claim is separate from, and in addition to, your claim for no-fault benefits.

Bodily injury coverage comes from the insurance company for the vehicle that was at fault for the accident. Your bodily injury and no-fault claims could both be paid by the same company, if the vehicle that you were in at the time of the accident was at fault, or if you were a pedestrian or bicyclist.

When you bring a lawsuit, you are generally seeking to recover money from the bodily injury coverage applicable to the vehicle that was at fault for the accident.

How to recover even if you were at fault for an accident.

After a motor vehicle accident, the police or witnesses may say that you were at fault. You may even have been given a ticket for the accident. This does not automatically mean that you are not entitled to benefits for injuries that you sustained.

1. Medical expenses and lost earnings

   If your accident occurs in a state that requires no-fault coverage, you are entitled to collect no-fault benefits for your medical bills and for some lost wages, even if you were at fault for the accident. No-fault gets its name because the insurance company cannot consider who is at fault when paying benefits.

   In states that do not have no-fault laws, often referred to as "tort states," you can often collect money for lost wages and medical expenses even if you contributed to causing the accident. This is because in most accidents, no one person is 100% at fault.

2. Pain, suffering, and permanent injuries

   Many states have laws that allow injured people to recover for pain, suffering, and permanent injuries, even if the injured person's own negligence partially contributed to the accident. Even if your conduct contributed to the accident, you may be able to bring a lawsuit to recover for such damages—because the other party may have contributed to causing the accident as well.

   For example, if you go through a red light and are involved in an accident, you are partially at fault. But it is possible that the other driver has some responsibility as well. The other driver may have seen you going through the red light, but made no effort to avoid you. The other driver's attention may have been distracted. The other driver may have been speeding or driving while intoxicated.

For purposes of this example, assume that you were 80% responsible for the accident and the other party was 20% responsible, and that the full value of your injuries is $100,000.00. The law in some states, including New York, would allow you to recover, but would reduce the value of your injuries by 80%—the amount that you were at fault for the accident. You would therefore be entitled to recover $20,000.00.

How to recover even if you receive a ticket for an accident

If you receive a ticket as a result of a motor vehicle accident, you may feel that the ticket is proof that you were at fault. But a ticket is not proof of fault. The police officer who issued the ticket probably did not see the accident happen. The ticket is probably based upon nothing more than the officer's opinion. Only a court can decide, after evidence is presented at a trial, if a ticket is valid.

Even if the charges contained in the ticket are proved to be true, they do not mean that you are completely at fault. The other driver's conduct may have also contributed to the accident.

In some states, a ticket from an accident cannot be used as evidence against you in your personal injury case unless you plead guilty to the ticket. If you enter a plea of guilty to the ticket, however, your guilty plea could be interpreted as a statement that you caused the accident. You should therefore never enter a guilty plea to any ticket received as a result of a motor vehicle accident without consulting an attorney.

What is underinsured motorist coverage?

Automobile insurance policies have limits as to how much money will be paid to compensate an injured person. These policy limits are sometimes insufficient. The injured person has no control over the policy limits available, since these are governed by the bodily injury coverage for the other driver—the at-fault party. Protection from the potentially inadequate policy limits of other drivers is available, however, in the form of underinsured motorist coverage.

Underinsured motorist coverage is coverage that you purchase from your own automobile insurance company. If your liability policy limits are greater than those of the other driver, your underinsured motorist coverage may be available to help compensate you for your injuries.

Some states require insurance agents to tell you about the availability of underinsured motorist coverage. If you have questions about whether you presently have such coverage, you should consult your attorney or insurance agent.

Things to do if you are injured in a motor vehicle accident.

1. Immediately call an ambulance if anyone is hurt. If you are injured, go immediately to the hospital or to your doctor.

2. Call the police to report the accident.

3. Wait for a police officer to arrive before moving any vehicles, unless leaving the vehicles will create a safety hazard. If vehicles are being moved, note their position before moving them.

4. Write down the name(s) of the driver and owner of the other vehicle, and the name of their insurance company.

5. Get the name, address and phone numbers of any witnesses.

6. Ask the other driver why he or she caused the accident (for example, "Why did you run the red light?").

7. Promptly notify your own insurance company of the accident.

8. If possible, obtain photographs of the damage to all vehicles.

9. Call a lawyer who is experienced with auto accident cases.

10. Never give a statement, sign anything or admit fault without first talking to a lawyer.

SLIP AND FALL ACCIDENTS

Generally speaking, property owners are required to keep their property in a reasonably safe condition and are required to provide warnings of any unsafe conditions. Failure to maintain property in a reasonably safe condition or to provide warnings of hazards may constitute negligence. If you sustain injuries as a result of such negligence, you may be able to bring a claim against the owner of the property.

A very important fact in any slip and fall accident is whether the property owner was aware of the hazard that caused your injury **before** your accident occurred. If the owner knew or should have known of the hazard, and failed to remove it or warn you of its existence, the property owner could be liable for your injuries.

There are many hazards which might cause or contribute to a slip and fall accident. These hazards include buildups of snow and ice on outdoor sidewalks; product spills in grocery stores; slippery floors, absence of handrails on stairs, and poor lighting. Any such conditions should be pointed out to the owner of the property where the fall occurred, as well as to any witnesses to the accident.

Witness statements are particularly important in slip and fall cases, so be sure to ask the names and addresses of anyone who saw the cause of your fall, or who may have reported the hazard to the property owner **before** you were injured. In addition, you should obtain and review a copy of any written accident report, which should include a description of the hazard and the names of all witnesses.

Some property owners have insurance that will pay for some of your medical expenses associated with a slip and fall accident. There is no guarantee, however, that any of your damages will be paid without commencing a lawsuit.

CONSTRUCTION AND OTHER WORK-RELATED ACCIDENTS

While laws applicable to construction and other work-related accidents vary from state to state, many states have enacted laws that protect workers who are injured while they are on the job. Workers' compensation, which is more fully discussed in Section Fourteen, provides one example of such laws. Workers' compensation benefits insure that all workers injured during the scope of their employment will receive compensation for lost earnings, and coverage for medical expenses associated with their injuries. These benefits are paid by the insurance company for the employer of the injured person. Therefore, the law prohibits the injured person from suing the employer for his or her injuries—even if the employer is completely responsible for causing the accident that resulted in those injuries.

But what if a worker was injured:

- in a car accident while on the way from the workplace to a business meeting

- in a fall caused by a buildup of ice and snow on the sidewalk of a building where they were making a delivery for their employer

- when their foot became trapped in a defective machine

- in a fall from an elevated height while performing construction work on an office building

In each of these examples, the injured worker may be able to collect workers' compensation **and** bring a lawsuit against someone other than their employer. Such lawsuits are sometimes referred to as "third party claims," because a third party (someone other than the employer) is being sued.

When an injured worker brings a third party claim, he or she will generally be required to reimburse workers compensation from the third party settlement proceeds for all benefits that compensation has paid. This requirement that workers compensation be repaid is called a lien. Liens are more fully discussed in Section Eleven.

Individuals who work in construction trades are particularly susceptible to work-related injuries, because construction work requires extreme physical exertion and often must be performed at elevated heights. Some states, such as New York, have enacted laws that furnish special protection for workers in construction trades.

This law requires property owners and general contractors to provide safety devices to workers who perform their jobs at elevated heights. The worker need only demonstrate that he or she fell from an elevated height and was injured while performing construction or repair work on a building or structure, and that safety devices such as ropes or harnesses were not furnished. If the worker can establish these points, he or she has proved that the owner of the property and/or general contractor for the job is responsible for the injuries sustained. Even if the worker's own conduct caused or contributed to the accident, such conduct may not be held against the worker. The only issue then left to be resolved is the value of the worker's injuries.

ACCIDENTS CAUSED BY DEFECTIVE PRODUCTS

If you are injured by a defective product, you may be entitled to compensation from the product's manufacturer or seller. Products have been found defective because of the way in which they were designed or manufactured, as well as the failure to provide instructions or warnings.

Before using any product, you should always read the instructions furnished by the product's manufacturer or seller. Follow these instructions as you use the product. Do not make alterations or repairs to the product except as directed by the manufacturer and/or seller's instructions. If you do not use the product as advised by the manufacturer, the manufacturer could raise such misuse as a defense against you, thereby minimizing or destroying the value of your claim.

If you sustain an injury due to a defective product, the product should be preserved and not altered in any way. You should retain the proof of purchase and any instruction booklet or warranty information that might have been delivered with the product. It is also important to obtain the names of witnesses to the event, as well as the name of the manufacturer and/or seller of the product involved.

Cases involving product defects should be investigated as soon as possible in order to properly preserve the evidence, identify the manufacturer or the product, and determine the length of time left to bring a lawsuit.

AIRCRAFT ACCIDENTS

It is hard to imagine a more grisly or frightening accident than an airplane crash. Whether the crash involves a commercial jetliner, a small plane or a helicopter, airplane crashes almost invariably result in fatalities and provoke a strong emotional response.

A myriad of potential explanations exist for why aircraft crash. Among the causes are:

- Poorly designed parts

- Improperly manufactured parts

- Structural defects in the aircraft

- Repairs not performed, or performed improperly

- Errors by flight crew and/or ground personnel

- Failure to perform maintenance needed for flight in foul weather

- Poor design of airport runways

- Overcrowding of aircraft in the skies and while awaiting takeoff

Of course, crashes have also occurred due to terrorist activity; the presence of a bomb or other explosive device on an aircraft speaks to inadequate security at the airport.

When crashes occur, government officials and members of the public alike want to know what went wrong. Members of the public generally assume that if a crash does not occur, all is well in the skies. But the Federal Aviation Administration

Factbook presents the alarming figures that during 1995 alone, there were:

Description of incident	Number of incidents
Near-midair collisions	241
Pilot deviations	1,227
Operational errors	772
Vehicle-pedestrian deviations	276
Runway incursions	249

With airline deregulation has come an increase in concern over the safety of the flying public. While deregulation spurred competition within the industry, it has simultaneously permitted airlines to operate "on a shoestring," luring travelers with inexpensive fares. Larger carriers, whose business is potentially threatened by these low-budget upstarts, are likewise tempted to economize. Some economy measures are merely annoying; others seriously compromise passengers' safety. Disaster can be the only result when airlines make profit, not safety, their primary goal.

At the end of this chapter, you will find a list of safety-related questions. Every major airline was sent this list of questions, and asked to respond. The airlines' responses are available to you by calling 1-800-546-7777.

At the end of this chapter, you will also find a list of important telephone numbers. These numbers are for various consumer and regulatory associations concerned with airline safety.

The following are commonly asked questions relating to crashes of aircraft and other claims based on aircraft safety:

Q. How many fatal transportation-related accidents occur each year?

A. The National Transportation Safety Board has compiled statistics on transportation fatalities in the United States. For 1995, these figures show:

Type of Transportation	Number of Fatalies
Highway	
Passenger cars	22,313
Pedestrians	5,620
Motorcycles	2,230
Buses	28
All other	<u>11,509</u>
Total Highway	41,700
Railroad	753
Marine	904
Aviation	
General aviation	732
Air taxi	52
Commuter	9
Foreign/unregistered	8
Airlines	<u>168</u>
Total Aviation	969
Pipeline	21
GRAND TOTAL	<u>44,247</u>

Q. What are some of the worst plane crashes that have occurred?

A. While every crash is a tragedy, those involving the most fatalities include:

Date	Description	Number of Fatalities
July 17, 1996	TWA Flight 800 exploded after takeoff from New York City	230
May 11, 1996	ValuJet DC-9 crashed in Florida Everglades	110

Jan. 8, 1996	Zairian Antonov-32 cargo plane crashed after takeoff from Kinshasa, Zaire; most fatalities were shoppers in market where plane crashed	350
Apr. 26, 1994	China Airlines Airbus crashed on landing at Nagoya, Japan airport	262
Sept. 8, 1994	US Air 737-400 crashed on approach to Pittsburgh airport	132
July 11, 1991	DC-8 crashed on takeoff from Mecca	261
Dec. 21, 1988	PanAm Airlines flight en route to New York from London exploded over Lockerbie, Scotland, due to terrorist bomb	270
July 3, 1988	Iran Air A300 Airbus shot down in error by U.S. Navy missile	290
Aug. 16, 1987	Northwest Airlines MD-80 crashed after takeoff from Detroit	156
Dec. 12, 1985	Arrow Air DC-8 crashed on takeoff from Gander, Newfoundland	256
Aug. 12, 1985	Japan Air Lines 747 crashed in flight from Tokyo to Osaka	520
Aug. 2, 1985	Delta Airlines TriStar crashed at landing due to wind shear at Dallas-Ft. Worth airport	133
June 23, 1985	Air India 747 exploded off coast of Ireland, due to suspected terrorist bomb	329
Sept. 1, 1983	Korean Airlines 747 shot down over Siberia by Soviet fighter jet after straying into Soviet airspace	269
July 9, 1982	PanAm Airlines 727 crashed after takeoff from New Orleans; fatalities included eight people who were killed on the ground	154

Aug. 19, 1980	Saudia Airlines TriStar caught fire during emergency landing at Riyadh, Saudi Arabia	301
Nov. 28, 1979	Air New Zealand DC-10 crashed over Antarctica	257
May 25, 1979	Engine of DC-10 fell off of plane on takeoff from Chicago's O'Hare airport	275
Sep. 25, 1978	Pacific Southwest 727 collided with small plane near San Diego; fatalities included seven people killed on the ground	144
March 27, 1977	Pan Am Airlines 747 collided with KLM 747 while on runway at airport in Tenerife, Canary Islands	588
June 24, 1975	Eastern Airlines 727 crashed while attempting to land at New York's JFK airport during storm	113
March 3, 1974	Turkish Airlines DC-10 crashed near Paris	346
Dec. 16, 1970	United Airlines DC-8 collided with TWA Super Constellation in mid-air over New York City; fatalities included 8 killed on the ground	135
June 30, 1956	United Airlines DC-7 collided with TWA Super Constellation over the Grand Canyon	128

Q. Bringing a case against an airline seems very complicated. How would I go about bringing a claim?

A. To someone who lacks experience or is not familiar with a particular area of law, any type of case can appear complicated. A lawyer who is aggressive and experienced in handling airplane crash cases and other types of mass disasters will know what sorts of claims to file on your behalf and what courts are the most advantageous for your claim.

Another important concern in selecting an attorney for a case of this type is the lawyer's ability to finance the litigation. The necessary investigation and expert witnesses to support your claim will be costly; most lawyers do not have the funds that are necessary to build up a case of this nature. To successfully bring an aircraft liability claim, your lawyer must have sufficient financial resources to devote to the case.

Q. Who can be sued for the crash of an aircraft?

A. Who will be sued depends on how and why the crash occurred. For example:

If the crash was due to poor maintenance, the probable defendants would be the airline and/or a company to which the airline subcontracted maintenance work.

If the crash resulted due to the inadequacy of the airport's facilities, such as runways being too short, a claim may potentially lie against the owner of the airport.

If the crash occurred because a part of the aircraft unexpectedly malfunctioned during flight, there may be a claim against the manufacturer of the part, the manufacturer of the aircraft, the airline, and the maintenance provider for the aircraft.

Since most airplane crashes result from a confluence of factors, claims may be brought against many parties in order to insure completeness in pursuing the litigation.

Q. Are there any limitations on how much I can recover if a loved one is killed in an airplane crash?

A. For domestic plane crashes, there is no legal limitation on the amount that can be recovered for compensatory damages. The law of some states may restrict the recovery of punitive damages.

For plane crashes that occur on non-domestic flights, the Warsaw Convention currently places a monetary limitation on claims, although there may be exceptions to such limitations. In such instances, your attorney should search for exceptions that will enable your recovery to be maximized.

In some instances, the amount available for recovery is limited, not by law, but by the policy limits of insurance that covers the airline. In one recent crash, only $750 million was available in insurance funds. The airline involved sought bankruptcy protection shortly after the crash.

Many survivors and families of those killed in airplane crashes will receive only around $1 million, yet some families have recovered in excess of $20 million. The best recoveries go to those who are aggressive; who do not wait for or rely on airlines or insurance companies to make a fair offer. To obtain the best recovery, your attorney must aggressively build up your case, including fully investigating the liability of all potential parties.

Remember, you can only settle a case once. Likewise, you have only one opportunity to present your case at trial. Your attorney must be aggressive to get the information that will motivate the other side to settle for a fair amount, or that will convince a jury of the value of your case.

Q. How can I be sure that I am flying on a plane that has been properly maintained?

A. Cost-cutting pressures have prompted many airlines to outsource maintenance work to independent contractors. Independent contractors are awarded maintenance contracts because they promise that they can perform the maintenance work more cheaply than the airline's own maintenance crews.

Such cost-cutting measures can have serious consequences. In order to get the job done cheaply and still make a profit, the independent contractor must hire workers at a low rate of pay—far lower than the union wages paid to most airline mechanics. Workers willing to work for low wages generally lack the education, skills and experience of those who can command higher compensation.

There have even been reports that workers hired by independent contractors cannot read or understand English—and thus cannot comprehend the technical manuals which detail the maintenance and repair work needed for a particular aircraft.

Aircraft repairs and maintenance are literally a life and death matter. When human lives hang in the balance, safety cannot be subordinated to cost. Airlines that invest adequate time and money in the training of maintenance and repair crews; that pay a fair wage to these workers; and that adjust flight schedules as needed to accommodate maintenance and repair work, offer the best alternative.

Q. How can it be proved that a crash occurred because of defective parts?

A. Federal officials, such as investigators from the National Transportation Safety Board and the Federal Aviation Administration, travel immediately to crash sites to investigate the scene and the wreckage. Scientific investigation can pinpoint structural weaknesses, defective parts and other mechanical difficulties. In addition, review of the information collected by the flight data recorders may provide investigators with clues about what went wrong.

Lawyers who are working for crash victims can also hire private investigators to develop the facts. These investigators will review the information gathered by the NTSB, FAA and other government authorities. In addition, they will gather more information to try and build up the claim—for example, evidence of conscious pain and suffering experienced by victims in the moments immediately prior to the crash.

Q. What are counterfeit parts?

A. Aircraft builders do not manufacture all of the component parts for planes or helicopters themselves. They contract with other companies, which build specialized parts that handle certain aircraft functions.

These component parts are required—by the aircraft manufacturer and, in some cases, by the Federal Aviation Administration—to meet certain technical specifications. Because of the technical expertise involved, only certain manufacturers are certified to make such parts.

Counterfeit parts are made to look like ones that are properly manufactured—even though they have been manufactured under much less exacting technical standards than the genuine parts. By using a complex web of distributors, suppliers, and other middlemen, parts counterfeiters have been able to fool even the most respected of aircraft makers.

Q. Can an airline be sued for using inappropriate or counterfeit parts in its aircraft?

A. Counterfeit parts seriously compromise the safety of the traveling public. If investigation discloses that counterfeit parts were used in an aircraft that has crashed, liability for damages, including punitive damages, could lie against the airline, the aircraft manufacturer and other individuals.

Q. What is wind shear?

A. Wind shear is a hazardous weather condition caused by rapid changes in wind currents. Wind shear has been blamed for the loss of hundreds of lives in plane crashes. The danger presented by wind shear is primarily during takeoff and landing.

When a plane meets a strong head wind, the plane takes a sudden leap in airspeed. The increase in airspeed lifts the plane. The pilot reduces engine power in response to this lifting. As the plane passes through the wind, a headwind may become a downdraft and then a tailwind. This shifting of wind causes a reduction in both the plane's speed and its altitude. If the pilot cannot increase engine power quickly enough to counteract the shifting winds, a crash will occur.

Q. What are my odds of being killed due to an aircraft crash?

A. In 1994, 30 commercial airplanes crashed, resulting in the loss of 264 lives. Statistically, this figure translates into the death of one out of every 1.7 million passengers. While these odds appear generally favorable to the air traveler, they must be assessed within a historical context. Over past decade, the odds of death from a plane crash have almost doubled—from one out of 3 million to the one in 1.7 million probability cited above for 1994.

Commuter airlines are by far the riskiest mode of air travel. Commuter lines are responsible for more than five times the number of accidents (rate per thousands) than commercial airlines. Some reasons behind the risk include:

- Commuter lines generally operate small planes, which are more vulnerable than jet airliners to adverse weather conditions.

- While jet planes can avoid poor weather by flying over or around it, most commuter planes must fly through storms.

- Commuter lines often serve as a training ground for pilots, who use the commuter line as a stepping stone to a career with a large airline. Less experienced pilots means a greater margin for error.

- Many commuter lines are operated by small, "upstart" companies, which do not have the financial resources of a large airline. This lack of resources can translate into less attention than needed to maintenance, repairs and other safety concerns.

Q. How old are the planes that are currently in service for major airlines?

A. In 1995, the National Institute for Aviation Research reported the average age of the planes flown by various airlines:

Airline	Age of Planes (in years)
Southwest	8.02
American	8.77
America West	9.46
Delta	10.41
United	11.18
USAir	11.58
Continental	14.47
Northwest	17.56
TWA	19.38

Q. How can I find an attorney who has the necessary experience and resources to bring a claim dealing with an aircraft crash?

A. Your claim will be against large corporations—such as aircraft manufacturers, airlines and their insurers. These companies may have billions of dollars in revenues—and they are willing to spend their money to fight against claimants. If your lawyer lacks vast financial resources to fight for your rights, your claim could be seriously compromised.

Your lawyer should be willing and able to spend up to one million dollars to prepare and try your case. Although many cases require less than this amount to be properly developed, your lawyer should be prepared for the worst case scenario. If your lawyer runs short of money at a critical time, you could effectively be forced to settle for an unfairly small amount.

When selecting your lawyer, you should recognize that most lawyers' practices are very specialized. Attorneys whose practices center on wills, divorces or real estate are unlikely to have the expertise needed to handle the complexities of an aircraft disaster claim. Your attorney should be an experienced litigator who is not afraid to go to court—someone who has years of experience in suing and recovering from large corporations and insurance companies.

AIRLINE SAFETY QUESTIONS

These questions were mailed to ten large airlines. You can call 1-800-546-7777 to request of a free copy of the airlines' responses:

1. What is the company's record regarding accidents and regulatory violations?

2. Who is responsible for aircraft repairs and maintenance? Please furnish the names and addresses of any independent contractors that are used.

3. Please list and describe all new or important safety equipment on your planes. Please specify the model and type of airplane for each item of safety equipment discussed..

4. What is the average age the planes in your fleet? Please detail the age of the planes by manufacturer and model.

5. What is the total number of hours flown in the past 12 months by all of your planes?

6. What hiring requirements does your company impose for pilots?

7. What safety courses must flight crews take, and how many hours each year of safety instruction must each flight crew member attend?

8. What was your company's total revenue for the past year?

9. How much of your company's total revenue was spent on safety for the past year?

10. Does your company carry liability insurance against crashes? How much insurance money is available for accidents or death resulting from a crash?

11. What safety devices have you installed on your planes to prevent wind shear accidents?

12. Do the warning lights on your planes flash at the levels required by the Federal Aviation Administration?

13. In the event of a crash on your airline, who should a passenger's family members contact to find out more information?

14. What safeguards does your company have in place to prevent purchasing and using counterfeit or faulty airplane parts?

15. Because safety is very important, we would welcome any additional comments that you may have regarding your company's philosophy regarding safety concerns.

IMPORTANT PHONE NUMBERS

Federal Aviation Administration Consumer Hotline: 1-800-322-7873. This FAA watchdog addresses complaints about airport security, carry-on baggage or the FAA itself

Safety Hotline: 1-800-255-1111. This hotline investigates reports of violations of federal airport and airplane regulations, as well as reports of unsafe situations involving airports or aircraft. Calling this hotline is often the first step for whistleblowers—those inside the aviation industry who want to call attention to illegal or unsafe practices.

International Airline Passengers Association: 1-214-404-9980. This association publishes and distributes bi-monthly travel safety alerts to approximately 150,000 members.

Aviation Consumer Action Project: 1-202-638-4000. Founded in 1971 by Ralph Nader, this organization researches aviation issues relevant to consumers and publishes facts and advice for airline passengers. The organization offers advice by telephone about passenger rights and aviation safety.

SECTION THREE

EXPOSURE TO TOXIC SUBSTANCES

ASBESTOS

Asbestos is a fibrous mineral that can be highly toxic when inhaled, absorbed, or otherwise ingested by the body. For many years, asbestos was a commonly used insulation material. Individuals who have worked in construction trades, manufacturing plants, railroads, and other occupations where insulation or construction materials are present may have been exposed to asbestos

Asbestos fibers, when taken into the body, can cause ailments including asbestosis, mesothelioma, and a number of cancers. Ordinarily, asbestos related health problems do not develop without extended exposure, but some individuals can develop problems based on exposures that are relatively limited.

Asbestos is generally regarded as most dangerous when it is airborne. If you encounter asbestos in your home or workplace, you should not remove it yourself. Professional asbestos abatement services are available, and such agencies should be consulted to ensure that the asbestos is removed and disposed of in a safe, environmentally sound manner.

If you believe that you have been exposed to asbestos and have sustained injuries as a result of such exposure, you may wish to seek legal counsel. Thousands of individuals have already recovered monies as a result of legal actions against the manufacturers of asbestos.

A wealth of information is available showing that the manufacturers of asbestos were aware of their products' highly toxic nature, and that these manufacturers chose to ignore such evidence when placing asbestos into the marketplace. Therefore, the primary burden on an individual who has been injured by asbestos in bringing legal action is to make sure that (1) his or her claim is timely filed and not barred by any applicable statute of limitations; and (2) to identify all asbestos containing products to which he or she was exposed.

Statutes of limitation, which are discussed more fully in Section Twelve, require that most legal cases be filed within a specified time. If you fail to file a case within the time specified by law, you will receive no recovery, regardless of the severity of your injuries. Statutes of limitation with regard to asbestos claims differ from state to state. Therefore, if you believe that you have been injured due to exposure to asbestos, you should contact an attorney immediately to learn what statute of limitation applies to your case.

Individuals who have been injured by exposure to asbestos must be able to identify products to which they were exposed in order to establish their right to recover against particular asbestos manufacturers. Product identification can be accomplished in a number of ways. For example, if you consult with an attorney with regard to a potential asbestos claim, you may be asked whether you remember the names of any products that were present in your workplace. Your attorney may ask you to review a book of photographs of various asbestos products, which may refresh your memory about what products were present at your jobsite. You may also be asked if you remember the names of any co-workers, supervisors, or other personnel from the companies, unions, or worksites where you were exposed. Even if you do not recall the names of asbestos products that were present, these individuals may remember, thereby establishing a link between particular products and your injuries. Further, such individuals or entities may have records of what supplies were ordered for particular jobsites.

If you were exposed to asbestos during the course of your employment, you may also be entitled to recover workers' compensation benefits for injuries that you have sustained.

Like statutes of limitation, workers' compensation laws vary from state to state. If you believe you have sustained an injury due to workplace exposure to asbestos, consultation with an attorney may assist you in clarifying your rights to recover workers' compensation, as well as other monies for your pain, suffering, and permanent injuries.

COMMON QUESTIONS ABOUT ASBESTOS

Q. I thought that all asbestos cases were over and done with. Hasn't all of the asbestos companies' money been given away? Why is it important to think about an asbestos claim now?

A. It is true that asbestos is no longer used in insulation or fireproofing products. But there is still time to bring an asbestos claim.

Asbestos damage takes a long time to develop. Even if you were exposed 30 years ago, the damage may only be showing up now.

Because asbestos damage can show up years after your exposure, it is important to monitor your condition by periodically having chest x-rays. If more than two years have passed since your last chest x-ray, you may wish to schedule a new x-ray to check for lung damage.

If you have been damaged by asbestos, you could be entitled to money to compensate for your injuries. Over five billion dollars is just waiting for victims injured by asbestos.....but you cannot receive a share of this money until you ask for it. *Making a claim is your key to getting a share of that money!*

Asbestos litigation is growing, and the courts are continually presented with new legal issues. For example, in the fall of 1996, the United States Supreme Court agreed to decide two new issues presented in asbestos claims.

The first issue involved class actions. Class actions gather similar claims together, and resolve all of those claims at the same time. In the case before the Supreme

Court, an asbestos maker wanted to settle all claims through a class action—even though some of the claims were very different from each other. The Supreme Court faced the decision as to whether such a class action was appropriate.

The second issue involved the claims of people who were exposed to asbestos, but who were not yet sick. These people were concerned that asbestos would make them ill in the future. The Supreme Court considered whether these people could bring claims for physical injuries that could develop in the future, and whether they could recover for their worries about their future health.

Q. What types of products contain asbestos?

A. A large variety of products that were used for fireproofing and insulation contained asbestos. For example:

> Asbestos pipe covering was used to insulate pipes in commercial, industrial, and manufacturing settings.

> Asbestos block was used to insulate furnaces, boilers, and steam locomotives.

> Asbestos brick was used in the construction of large furnaces, such as those used in steel and other heat-intensive industries.

> Asbestos cement and sealants were generally used as mortar for asbestos brick, and to adhere other asbestos products to surfaces.

> Asbestos floor and ceiling tiles were used in construction projects, both commercial and residential.

> Asbestos fireproofing was sprayed on the framework for commercial buildings under construction.

Asbestos cloth, ropes, gaskets, blankets, and protective garments were used in a wide variety of industrial and manufacturing environments where intense heat and/or fireproofing was needed.

Q. What are the names of the companies that made asbestos products?

A. A list of many asbestos companies and some of the products that they made is included at the end of this section.

Q. How long does it take to bring a case against asbestos companies?

A. It is impossible to predict the length of any case. Attorneys have an obligation to do everything possible to get the best results for their clients. Most of the asbestos makers fight hard to avoid paying for the damage that their products caused.

When the asbestos makers fight hard, the attorney for the injured workers must fight back even harder. While it may take a long time—sometimes years—to fight the asbestos companies, getting the best result for the client makes the effort worthwhile.

Q. How many companies are sued in a typical asbestos case?

A. Every case is different, and the number of companies sued depends largely on the injured person's work history. Approximately 30 companies are sued in cases involving industrial exposure (such as steel mills, foundries, glass factories, and commercial construction).

Q. Is it possible to settle out of court?

A. Some asbestos companies may be willing to work toward fair settlements at an early point in the case. These companies have made the business decision that it is easier and less expensive to settle than to fight. Companies that are willing to enter into these settlements generally made products that were not widely used and/or did not create a large amount of asbestos dust.

Since it would be difficult to present enough evidence at trial to support liability against these companies, entering into settlements is often an attractive idea for both sides. The companies avoid expensive, time-consuming litigation.. The injured workers receive money early in the case, and are also saved the expense and time of pursuing "minor players."

Q. Does every person receive their settlement money at the same time?

A. Some companies will pay settlements to every person at the same time. Due to budgeting concerns, other companies may issue settlement payments in installments, over a period of time. For example, a settlement may cover 1,000 people and be paid over the course of 20 months. Every month, 50 more people will receive their settlement money. When an asbestos company pays a settlement in installments, the company, not the attorney for the injured workers, usually decides which clients will receive their money first.

Q. What will I have to do to get the settlement money?

A. Most settlements will require you to sign a document showing that you were exposed to the products of the company offering the settlement. This document is usually a written affidavit. The settling company will also require your signature on a release, a document that states that your claim against that company will end forever when you receive your money.

Sample forms of an affidavit and a release appear at the end of this section. *Please do not try to use these forms on your own!* You could lose all of your rights to recover money from a company if you try to negotiate a settlement without the help of a lawyer.

Q. I know that I worked with and around asbestos, but I do not remember the names of any specific products. Can I still bring a case?

A. You can bring a claim, even if you do not remember the names of specific products to which you were exposed. There are other ways to prove what products were present. For example:

> Your co-workers may remember details about the products. Since each person's memory may supply a new piece of information, the more co- workers that we can gather from a particular job site, the better an opportunity we have to identify products.
>
> Records maintained by your employer may show what asbestos products were present at your jobsite.
>
> Asbestos makers may have records showing that their products were purchased by particular employers.
>
> Wholesalers or suppliers may have records showing that your employer purchased certain brands of asbestos products.

All of these pieces of information can come together to furnish a complete picture of the products that were present where you worked.

Q. I worked around asbestos, but the air did not appear dusty. Could I have been damaged by asbestos?

A. Asbestos dust need not be visible to the naked eye to cause harm. Some scientific research suggests that invisible asbestos particles are more harmful than particles that can be seen. If you worked around asbestos—even if you could not see its dust—you may have inhaled microscopic asbestos particles.

Q. My primary care doctor recently asked me to get a chest x-ray. My doctor did not find any evidence of asbestos-related disease, even though I worked extensively with asbestos. Should I have another x-ray?

A. A new x-ray may be of benefit to you. To find asbestos damage, you must have a special type of x-ray, called a "PA view." Not every chest x-ray is a PA view.

Once you have obtained a PA view chest x-ray, a doctor qualified to diagnose asbestos damage must read the film. The doctor must be a radiologist who has received additional, specialized training in recognizing occupational disease. A radiologist who specializes in this area is called a "B-reader."

Unless your doctor obtained a PA view x-ray and sent it to a qualified B-reader for interpretation, your doctor may not be aware of the damage caused by asbestos.

Q. How will I know if my x-ray is positive for asbestos damage?

A. After interpreting the PA view x-ray, the B-reader will provide a report of the results. Different notations on the report indicate various types of damage caused by asbestos, as well as different levels of severity. The report may also discuss other lung abnormalities disclosed on the x-ray.

Once you have obtained a PA view x-ray and an interpretation of that film by a B-reader, you should share the B-reader's report with your own doctor. Your doctor will be able to explain the report to you. Once your doctor has read the report and explained it to you, he or she can make recommendations to safeguard your health.

Q. I obtained an x-ray, and it shows that I have asbestos damage. Does this mean that I am very ill or am going to die in the near future?

A. Knowing that you have tested positive for asbestos can be very frightening. It is impossible to predict the impact of your asbestos-related condition on your overall health.

The best source of information is your primary care physician and/or a physician who specializes in lung disorders. We strongly recommend that you share the results of your asbestos x-ray with your physician. Once your physician knows of your asbestos-related condition, he or she can take action as needed to protect your health.

Q. I smoked cigarettes for many years. I also worked around asbestos. Can I bring an asbestos claim, even though cigarettes also cause damage to the lungs?

A. Even if you were or are a smoker, you can still bring an asbestos claim. Medical experts can generally distinguish the damage caused by asbestos from that caused by smoking.

Q. Each day, my wife laundered my work clothes, which were dusty from asbestos. This was my wife's only asbestos exposure. Should she have an x-ray to screen for asbestos-related disease?

A. Although the possibility cannot be entirely ruled out, such limited exposure is unlikely to result in asbestos-related disease. Unless your wife is suffering from a breathing problem that is not due to any other illness, it is not recommend that she obtain an x-ray to screen for asbestos related disease.

Q. I did not work on any jobs where asbestos was present, but I performed home improvement projects in which I worked around asbestos. Should I have an x-ray?

A. While asbestos related disease cannot be ruled out based on a limited exposure, it is unlikely that brief home improvement projects would result in an asbestos related disease.

Q. How long do I have to bring as asbestos case?

A. Under New York law, the statute of limitations (time limit) for bringing a claim generally begins to run from the date that you learn you are suffering from an asbestos related disease. Remember, however, that each case is different, and that the laws of every state determine statutes of limitation based on different factors.

It is impossible to determine the length of time available in individual cases without a thorough review of the facts. To learn how long you have to bring a claim, you should consult with an attorney.

Q. How much money can I expect to receive if I bring an asbestos case?

A. Since each case is different, it is impossible to predict how much money would be awarded in any individual case. The amount that you might receive depends on a variety of factors including:

The location where you worked;

The type of work that you performed;

The products that you worked with or around;

The years of your exposure;

The severity of your injuries; and

How those injuries have affected your life.

Q. I want to pursue a claim, but I am uncomfortable with the prospect of having to testify in court. Is it always necessary to go to trial?

A. Most cases are settled out of court, without the need for a trial. The large number of cases makes it impossible for the asbestos makers to conduct trials on all but a very few cases. Even cases that proceed to trial are often settled before the jury reaches a verdict.

Q. What happens to my case if I die before settlement or trial?

A. If you die during the course of your case, the case can continue. A legal representative will be appointed—usually your spouse, one of your children, or another close relative. If you have a will, you can name the person who you want to serve as your legal representative. Settlement proceeds received after your death will be distributed by your legal representative, as specified by law, to your survivors or beneficiaries. In most states, including

New York, a judge supervises the distribution of settlement proceeds.

Q. What will I have to do if I decide to pursue a claim?

A. Because you (and your co-workers) are a valuable source of information, you will be asked many questions about the type of work that you performed, the location where you worked, and what you remember about the products that you used. You may also be asked questions about your health history and your personal background. You must always try to respond thoroughly and accurately to such questions, since they are important to your case.

You may be asked to review and sign papers that will allow your attorney to obtain your medical records, x-rays, and employment information.

Your attorney may prepare affidavits for your signature, if you have been exposed to particular products, and can remember details about those products. Such affidavits will help to develop your case and the cases of your co-workers. You may also need to sign certain documents associated with the litigation process, and with settlements.

You may also be asked to give a deposition. At the deposition, you will answer questions under oath about your work history, product exposure, and injuries. Depositions are generally held in an attorney's office, and the only people present are your own attorney, the attorneys representing the asbestos makers, and a stenographer who will write down everything that is said. The most important rule for giving any deposition is to be honest.

Q. What does an asbestos lawsuit look like?

A. Copies of a sample Summons and Complaint (the documents that begin a lawsuit) are included at the end of this section.

When reviewing the Summons and Complaint, please remember that they are general forms, which are used as guides. When preparing the Summons and Complaint for your case, your attorney will tailor the form (for example, by adding or removing asbestos companies) so that it reflects the facts of your individual case.

Please do not attempt to use these forms to begin a lawsuit on your own! Asbestos litigation is very complicated. There are special rules that must be followed to begin and proceed with a case. If you try to bring a case without the help of an attorney who knows all of these rules, your case could be dismissed—which means that your case would be over for good, before you received any money.

Q. An earlier question and answer discussed the sorts of information that I will have to provide in connection with my case. Specifically, what information is required?

A. Most of the information that will be needed is encompassed by a legal document called Interrogatories. "Interrogatories" is just a fancy word for "questions."

The attorneys for the asbestos companies will send your attorney the Interrogatories—a list of written questions. Your attorney will write proposed answers to all of these questions. Your lawyer will then send you both the questions and the proposed answers for you to review.

When reviewing your Interrogatories, pay close attention! You will sign the Interrogatories, and swear that all of the answers are the truth. Your answers to these questions are just as important as any testimony that you might give at a deposition or at a trial in court.

Sample Interrogatories are provided at the end of this section. Just as with the sample Complaint, you should not attempt to use the sample Interrogatories to pursue a case without an attorney. Your attorney will know the best way to answer the questions.

The questions asked in Interrogatories may differ from one case to another. Some courts require that all clients answer a standard form of Interrogatories. Your attorney will obtain the correct form of Interrogatories.

Q. I have heard of many class actions involving asbestos products. What is the difference between proceeding with a class action and pursuing an individual lawsuit?

A. Class actions are lawsuits on behalf of many injured people. The claims of the injured people are similar, and are generally made against only one or a few asbestos makers. Class actions can help asbestos companies to settle many claims at the same time.

An individual lawsuit is personalized. It is your own claim for injuries against many companies that could be responsible for your asbestos damage.

You can participate in class actions regarding some companies, and still pursue an individual lawsuit against others.

Some class actions may work to your benefit by offering a settlement that makes economic sense. Other class actions may offer you a settlement that is too low. You should never accept a class action settlement without consulting with an attorney.

If your attorney finds that the class action does not offer you enough settlement money, your attorney may recommend that you "opt out" of the class action. Your attorney will then pursue an individual lawsuit on your behalf against the company or companies involved in the class action.

If your attorney concludes that participation in a class action settlement is beneficial, he or she should prepare all of the necessary documents to qualify you for settlement money.

Q. Isn't it true that many manufacturers of asbestos have declared bankruptcy?

A. Some asbestos manufacturers have sought Chapter 11 bankruptcy protection. Included among these companies is Johns Manville, one of the largest manufacturers of asbestos products.

Q. If I was exposed to products of a bankrupt company, does this mean that I will not receive any money for my injuries?

Contrary to popular belief, filing for bankruptcy does not necessarily mean that a company has no money. Typically, asbestos companies file for bankruptcy to protect themselves from large numbers of claims. If the company paid all of the claims at the same time, it would run out of money. If the company can spread out payments, it will more likely be able to pay all of the people who have suffered injuries.

Filing for bankruptcy stays (places "on hold") the lawsuits against the company. While the lawsuits are stayed, the Bankruptcy Court formulates a plan for the company's reorganization. As part of this plan, the Bankruptcy Court will institute a program for payment of claims brought by injured people.

Typically, more severe claims, such as those on behalf of people who are dying from their asbestos-related illness, are given priority for payment. Other claims are generally paid on a "first come-first served" basis.

Q. Have all of the asbestos makers filed for bankruptcy?

A. Many companies involved in the sale and distribution of asbestos remain financially solvent. Examples of such companies include Owens Corning Fiberglass, Owens-Illinois, General Electric, Babcock & Wilcox, Combustion Engineering, Georgia-Pacific, Pittsburgh Plate Glass, Uniroyal, Westinghouse, and WR Grace. Lawsuits may proceed in court against these and many other companies.

Q. I do not want to sue my employer. Can I bring a claim that does not involve my employer?

A. Your claim is against the makers of asbestos products—not against your employer.

The law in many states, including New York, prohibits an injured employee from suing his or her employer.

Q. Can all of the people who belonged to a particular union, or all of the people who worked together at a certain jobsite, bring a case through the same attorney?

A. People who worked in the same trades or at the same jobsites can reap tremendous benefits from working with the same attorney. When an attorney represents a large group of people who worked in a particular trade or at a particular site, the attorney has access to more sources of information about the asbestos products that were present. In turn, this information helps to build up and strengthen each individual's claim.

When many cases move forward together, the combined force of those claims often motivates the asbestos companies to offer fair settlements.

REPRESENTATIVE ASBESTOS MAKERS AND PRODUCTS

Company Name	Representative Products
A. P. Green Company	Pipe covering, insulation adhesive, insulation block, refractory castables, insulating and finishing cements
A. W. Chesterton	Sheeting, steam valve packing, gaskets and gasket tape
AC& S Co.	Spray insulation
Anchor Packing	Gaskets, gasket sheets, and gasket tape; braided packing; compressed sheet packing
Armstrong World Industries	Pipe covering and insulation, block, cements, gaskets, cellulose, ceiling tile, paper, spray insulation
Babcock & Wilcox	Spray insulation, mortar, furnace lining, blankets, bulk fiber, cement, rope, rollboard
Philip Carey Manufacturing Co.	Pipe covering and insulation, cements, cement board, block
Combustion Engineering, Inc.	Pipe covering, block, cements, board, rope, gaskets, blankets, cloth

Flintkote	Car cement, insulating coating, asbestos cement pipe, joint cement
GAF Corporation	Pipe covering, block, felt, insulation cement, floor tile, millboard, siding, and shingles
Garlock, Inc.	Block cement, asbestos sheet, packing material
General Electric	Insulated cable and wire, paper
Georgia Pacific	Joint compound, patching plaster, drywall adhesive, spackling compound, topping compound
Kaiser Aluminum & Chemical Corp.	Metal cased brick, finishing cement, block, plastic insulation
Keasbey & Mattison (also see Turner & Newall)	Cements, cement pipe, fiber
M. H. Detrick Co.	Asbestos board, mineral wool cement, fireproofing cement
National Gypsum	Cements, cement siding, cement board, cement panels, topping, jackets for pipe covering, stripping tape, plaster, joint compound, laminating adhesive, paints,

	spray-on acoustical plaster and textures, ceiling panels
Owens Corning Fiberglass Corp.	Kaylo board, pipe insulation and covering (Kaylo & Unibestos), block (Kaylo & Unibestos)
Pfizer Minerals	Talc
Pittsburgh Corning Corp.	Unibestos block, pipe covering, insulation
Quigley Co., Inc.	Joint sealant, refractory and waterproof cements
Rutland Fire Clay	Cement, concrete, paints
Turner & Newall (also see Keasbey & Mattison)	Finishing cement, pipe insulation, block, cloth, rope packing, tape
U. S. Mineral	Spray, patch fiber
Uniroyal Inc.	Compressed asbestos sheet packing
United States Gypsum	Acoustical spray and plaster, roofing, shingles, insulation block, fiber plaster, spray texture, drywall surfacer, paints, wallboard, vinyl
W. R. Grace	Zonolite board texture, acoustical plaster, cement, spray insulation; paper, tape, joint sealing com-

pound, bonding agent, masonry coating, drying ovens

Westinghouse Electric   Paper laminate for electrical equipment

SUPREME COURT
COUNTY OF [*county of venue*]   STATE OF NEW YORK

JOHN DOE and MARY DOE
              Plaintiff(s),

-VS-   **SUMMONS**

                            Index No.

A,C&S, INC.,
THE ANCHOR PACKING COMPANY,
ASARCO, INCORPORATED,
THE CARBORUNDUM COMPANY,
DRESSER INDUSTRIES, INC.,
FERRO CORPORATION,
FOSECO, INC.,
FOSTER WHEELER CORPORATION,
FOSTER WHEELER ENERGY CORPORATION,
GARLOCK INC.,
GENERAL ELECTRIC COMPANY,
GENERAL REFRACTORIES COMPANY,
HARBISON WALKER REFRACTORIES CO.,
LAKE ASBESTOS OF QUEBEC, LTD.,
METROPOLITAN LIFE INSURANCE CO.,
MINNESOTA MINING AND MANUFACTURING,
NORTH AMERICAN REFRACTORIES COMPANY,
OWENS-CORNING FIBERGLAS CORPORATION,
OWENS ILLINOIS, INC.,
PITTSBURGH CORNING CORPORATION,
PPG INDUSTRIES, INC.,
RAPID-AMERICAN CORPORATION,
UNIROYAL, INC.,
U.S. MINERAL PRODUCTS COMPANY,

**WESTINGHOUSE ELECTRIC CORPORATION,
WHEELER PROTECTIVE APPAREL,
W.R. GRACE & CO.-CONN.,**

Defendants.

Plaintiff designates [*county of venue*] as the place of trial. The basis of the venue is [*basis for venue*].

To the above named Defendants:

YOU ARE HEREBY SUMMONED to answer the complaint in this action and to serve a copy of your answer, or, if the complaint is not served with this summons, to serve a notice of appearance on the Plaintiff's attorney within **20** days after the service of this summons, exclusive of the day of service (or within 30 days after the service is complete if this summons is not personally delivered to you within the State of New York); and in case of your failure to appear or answer, judgment will be taken against you by default for the relief demanded in the Complaint.

DATED: [*date*]   SHAPIRO & SHAPIRO
                                   Attorneys for Plaintiff
                                   1820 First Federal Plaza
                                   Rochester, New York 14614
                                   (716) 262-6350

DEFENDANTS' ADDRESSES:

A, C & S CORPORATION
Serve: President/CEO
          120 North Lime Street
          Lancaster, PA 17603-2951

THE ANCHOR PACKING COMPANY
Serve: CT Corporation Systems
2 Peachtree Street
Atlanta, GA 30383

ASARCO INCORPORATED
Serve: The Corporation Trust
1209 Orange Street
Wilmington, Delaware 19801-1120

THE CARBORUNDUM COMPANY,
n/k/a Uniflax Corporation a/k/a Uniflax Corp.

Serve: 2351 Whirpool Street
Niagara Falls, NY 14302

DRESSER INDUSTRIES, INC.
Serve: CT Corporation Systems
Bank One Center, Suite 1600
707 Virginia Street East
Charleston, WV 25301-2723

FERRO CORPORATION
Serve: CT Corporation Systems
1633 Broadway
New York City, New York 10019-6708

FOSECO, INC.
Serve: CT Corporation Systems
PO Box 951
Charleston, WV 25323-0951

FOSTER WHEELER CORPORATION
Serve: President/CEO
666 Fifth Avenue
New York, NY 10103-0001

FOSTER WHEELER ENERGY CORPORATION

Serve: President/CEO
   666 Fifth Avenue
   New York, NY 10103-0001

GARLOCK, INC.

Serve: CT Corporation Systems
   1633 Broadway
   New York, NY 10019-6708

GENERAL ELECTRIC COMPANY

Serve: CT Corporation Systems
   PO Box 951
   Charleston, WV 25323-0951

GENERAL REFRACTORIES COMPANY

Serve: 225 City Line Avenue
   Bala Cynwd, PA 19004

HARBISON WALKER REFRACTORIES CO.

Serve: CT Corporation Systems
   815 Superior Avenue East Suite 1420
   Cleveland, OH 44114-2700

LAKE ASBESTOS OF QUEBEC, LTD.

Serve: President/CEO
   180 Maiden Lane, 25th Floor
   New York City, NY 10038-4925

METROPOLITAN LIFE INSURANCE CO.

Serve: One Madison Avenue
   New York, NY 10010-3605

MINNESOTA MINING AND MANUFACTURING COMPANY

Serve: CT Corporation Systems
   PO Box 951
   Charleston, WV 25323-0951

NORTH AMERICAN REFRACTORIES CO.

Serve: CT Corporation Systems
1633 Broadway
New York, NY 10019-6708

OWENS-CORNING FIBERGLAS CORPORATION

Serve: President/CEO
National Bank Building
608 Madison Avenue
Toledo, OH 43604-1108

OWENS ILLINOIS, INC.

Serve: CT Corporate Systems
1633 Broadway
New York, NY 10019-6708

PITTSBURGH CORNING CORP.

Serve: CT Corporate Systems
815 Superior Avenue East Suite 1420
Cleveland, OH 44114-2700

PPG INDUSTRIES, INC.

Serve: 500 Central Avenue
Albany, NY 12206-2213

RAPID-AMERICAN CORPORATION

Serve: 667 Madison Avenue
New York, NY 10021-8029

UNIROYAL, INC.

Serve: 500 Central Avenue
Albany, NY 12206-2213

U.S. MINERAL PRODUCTS CO.

Serve: President/CEO
Furnace Street
Stanhope, NJ 07874-2623

WESTINGHOUSE ELECTRIC CORPORATION

Serve: Prentice Corp.
1600 Laidley Tower
Charleston, WV 25301-2189

WHEELER PROTECTIVE APPAREL

Serve: Hudson Wheeler, President
2116 Middleford
Northfield, IL 60093-1121

W.R. GRACE CO.-CONN.

Serve: One Tower Center Road
Boca Raton, FL 33486-1010

<hr>

SUPREME COURT
COUNTY OF [*county of venue*]   STATE OF NEW YORK

JOHN DOE and MARY DOE,

          Plaintiff(s),

-VS-   **COMPLAINT**

                             Index No.

A,C&S, INC.,
THE ANCHOR PACKING COMPANY,
ASARCO, INCORPORATED,
THE CARBORUNDUM COMPANY,
DRESSER INDUSTRIES, INC.,
FERRO CORPORATION,
FOSECO, INC.,
FOSTER WHEELER CORPORATION,
FOSTER WHEELER ENERGY CORPORATION,
GARLOCK INC.,
GENERAL ELECTRIC COMPANY,
GENERAL REFRACTORIES COMPANY,
HARBISON WALKER REFRACTORIES CO.,
LAKE ASBESTOS OF QUEBEC, LTD.,
METROPOLITAN LIFE INSURANCE CO.,
MINNESOTA MINING AND MANUFACTURING,
NORTH AMERICAN REFRACTORIES COMPANY,
OWENS-CORNING FIBERGLAS CORPORATION,
OWENS ILLINOIS, INC.,
PITTSBURGH CORNING CORPORATION,
PPG INDUSTRIES, INC.,
RAPID-AMERICAN CORPORATION,
UNIROYAL, INC.,
U.S. MINERAL PRODUCTS COMPANY,

WESTINGHOUSE ELECTRIC CORPORATION, WHEELER PROTECTIVE APPAREL, W.R. GRACE & CO.-CONN.,

Defendants.

The plaintiffs, by their attorneys, Shapiro & Shapiro, complain of the defendants as follows:

1. The plaintiffs are residents of the County of [*county of residence*], State of New York.

2. The defendants are corporations, some of which are New York corporations, and some of which have offices and conduct business in the County of Niagara, State of New York.

3. All of the defendants are either licensed and registered corporations or business entities.

4. [*injured plaintiff's name*], the injured plaintiff, was exposed to asbestos and other harmful dusts in New York and/or was exposed to asbestos dust and other harmful products as the result of the manufacture, sale, distribution and installation of these products by the defendants in New York.

5. As a result of the plaintiff's exposure to asbestos and other harmful dusts in New York and/or his exposure to asbestos dust and other harmful products he has sustained serious personal injuries.

6. The plaintiff's injuries and their cause were discovered, through the plaintiff's exercise of reasonable diligence, on or about [*date that injury was discovered*]. Prior to that time, the state of medical, technical, and scientific knowledge was insufficient to ascertain the plaintiff's injuries or their cause.

7. Unless specifically stated otherwise, all causes of action stated herein are claimed against all defendants.

FIRST CAUSE OF ACTION—NEGLIGENCE

8. Over the course of his working years, the plaintiff worked with and/or around products containing asbestos and/or other harmful minerals manufactured, supplied, sold, distributed and installed by the defendants. As a result, the plaintiff breathed asbestos and other harmful dusts created by the use of said products, and developed serious, permanent and disabling lung disease.

9. The defendants and/or their agents, servants and employees were negligent, in that they knew or should have known that the use of their products would cause serious lung diseases and cancer, and knowing the same, failed to take reasonable precautions to warn the plaintiff of the dangers to which he was exposed; failed to inform the plaintiff of what would be safe and sufficient wearing apparel and safety equipment for persons who were exposed to their products; failed to properly and adequately label the products; sold products which were not in a reasonably safe condition; failed to supply accurate and complete warnings of the known dangers involved in the use of and exposure to the products; failed to use safe, substitute products when such were available; and negligently installed the products without taking precautions to warn and protect the plaintiff.

10. As a direct and proximate result of the negligence of the defendants which caused him to develop serious, permanent and disabling lung disease, the plaintiff suffered damages including but not limited to, medical expenses; great pain of body and mind; embarrassment; inconvenience; loss of wages and wage earning capacity; loss of quality and enjoyment of life; shortening of his life expectancy; increased risk

of cancer, asbestosis, mesothelioma, and other diseases related to exposure to asbestos, with the worry and concern that naturally flows from such increased risk; and permanent and disabling injury.

11. Such actions and failure to act on the part of the defendants constitutes malicious, willful and wanton misconduct with complete disregard for the safety and rights of others, amounting to extraordinary and outrageous conduct, especially when the defendants were aware of scientific and medical data made available to them that their products were harmful and deadly to workers who were exposed to them. The malicious, willful, and wanton acts and omissions of the defendants justify the imposition of punitive damages.

SECOND CAUSE OF ACTION—STRICT LIABILITY

12. The plaintiff incorporates by reference, as if fully set forth herein the allegations contained in paragraphs 1 through 11.

13. At the time the defendants placed their products on the market, such products contained defects which created an unreasonable risk of harm to those likely to use or be exposed to the product, including: (a) exposure to the product caused cancer and lung diseases, and (b) no warning or an inadequate warning was given to users or persons exposed to the product.

14. At the time of the plaintiff's exposure, the products were being used for the purposes for which they were intended, the products were in substantially the same condition as when they left the control of each of the defendants, and the plaintiff had no knowledge of the defects and no reason to suspect a defective condition.

15. As a sole, direct and proximate result of the defective products manufactured, supplied and sold by the defendants,

the plaintiff developed severe, permanent and disabling lung diseases and suffered the damages and losses enumerated in the First Cause of Action.

THIRD CAUSE OF ACTION—FRAUD

16. The plaintiff incorporates by reference, as if fully set forth herein the allegations contained in paragraphs 1–15.

17. The plaintiff was employed in capacities which placed him in close proximity with asbestos and asbestos-related materials, manufactured and/or distributed by the defendants. The plaintiff's presence was known or should have been known to the defendants and each of them.

18. The plaintiff was exposed to the asbestos products manufactured and/or distributed by one or more of the defendants named in paragraph 19. The exposure to the asbestos or asbestos-related product manufactured and/or distributed by the defendants proximately contributed to the disease suffered by the plaintiff as described below.

19. The defendants, as specifically identified below, individually and as agents of one another and as co-conspirators, agreed and conspired among themselves and with other asbestos manufacturers and distributors to injure the plaintiff in the following fashion:

(a) Beginning in approximately 1934, conspirator Johns-Manville Corporation, through its agents, Vandiver Brown and attorney J.C. Hobart, and conspirator Raybestos-Manhattan, through its agents, Sumner Simpson and J. Rohrbach, suggested to Dr. Anthony Lanza, Associate Director, Metropolitan Life Insurance Company (insurers of Manville and Raybestos), that Lanza publish a study on asbestosis in which Lanza would affirmatively misrepresent a material fact about asbestos exposure; that is the seriousness of the disease process, asbestosis. This was accomplished through intentional deletion of Lanza's description of asbestosis as "fatal" and through other selective editing that affirmatively misrepresented asbestos as a disease process less serious than it actually is and was known to be then. As a result, Lanza's study was published in the medical literature in this misleading fashion in 1935. The conspirators were motivated, in part, to effectuate this fraudulent misrepresentation and fraudulent nondisclosure by the desire to influence proposed legislation to regulate asbestos exposure and to provide a defense in lawsuits involving Manville, Raybestos and Metropolitan Life, as insurer.

(b) In 1936, conspirators American Brake Block Corporation, Asbestos Manufacturing Company, Gatke Corporation, Johns-Manville Corporation, Keasby & Mattison Company (then an alter-ego to conspirator Turner & Newall), Raybestos-Manhattan, Russell Manufacturing (whose liabilities have been assumed by H.K. Porter Company), Union Asbestos and Rubber Company and United States Gypsum Company, entered into an agreement with the Saranac Laboratories. Under this agreement, these conspirators acquired the power to decide what information Saranac Laboratories could publish about asbestos disease and could also control in what form such publications were to occur. This agreement gave these conspirators power to affirmatively misrepresent the results of the work at Saranac, and also gave these conspirators power to suppress material facts included in any study. On numerous occasions thereafter, the conspirators exercised their power to prevent Saranac scientists from disclosing material scientific data, resulting in numerous misstatements of fact being made at scientific meetings.

(c) On November 11, 1948, representatives of the following conspirators met at the headquarters of Johns-Manville Corporation: American Brake Block Division of American Brake and Shoe Foundry, Gatke Corporation, Keasby & Mattison Company (then an alter-ego to conspirator Turner & Newall), Raybestos-Manhattan, Inc., Thermoid Company (whose assets and liabilities were later purchased by H.K. Porter Company), Union Asbestos and Rubber Company and United States Gypsum Company. U.S. Gypsum did not send a representative to the meeting, but instead authorized Vandiver Brown of Johns-Manville to represent its interest at the meeting and to take action on its behalf.

(d) At this November 11, 1948, meeting, these defendants and their representatives decided to exert their influence to materially alter and misrepresent material facts about the substance of research started by Dr. Leroy Gardner at the Saranac Laboratories beginning in 1936. Dr. Gardner's research involved the carcinogenicity of asbestos in mice and also included an evaluation of the health effects of asbestos on humans with a critical review of the then-existing standards of dust exposure for asbestos and asbestos products.

(e) At this meeting, these defendants intentionally and affirmatively determined that Dr. Gardner's work should be edited to specifically delete material facts about the cancer-causing propensity of asbestos and the health effects of asbestos on humans and the critique of the dust standards and then published same in the medical literature as edited by Dr. Vorwald. These defendants thereby fraudulently misrepresented the risks of asbestos exposure to the public, in general, and the class of persons exposed to asbestos, including the plaintiff.

(f) As a direct result of influence exerted by the above-described conspirators, Dr. Vorwald published Dr. Gardner's edited work in the *Journal of Industrial Hygiene, AMA Archives of Industrial Hygiene and Occupational Health* in 1951, in a form that stressed those portions of Dr.

Gardner's work that the conspirators wished stressed, but which omitted references to human asbestosis and cancer, thereby fraudulently and affirmatively misrepresenting the extent of the risks. The conspirators affirmatively and deliberately disseminated this misleading Vorwald publication to university libraries, government officials, agencies and others.

(g) Such action constituted a material affirmative misrepresentation of the total context of material facts involved in Dr. Gardner's work and resulted in creating an appearance that inhalation of asbestos was less of a health problem than Dr. Gardner's unedited work indicated.

(h) The following conspirators were members of the trade association known as Quebec Asbestos Mining Association (Q.A.M.A.): Johns-Manville Corporation, Carey-Canada, individually and as successor to Quebec Asbestos Corporation, the Celotex Corporation, successor to Quebec Asbestos Corporation, National Gypsum Company, and Turner & Newall, individually and successor to Bell Asbestos and Asarco. Asarco acted through Lake Asbestos. These conspirators, members of Q.A.M.A., participated in the above-described misrepresentation of the work of Dr. Leroy Gardner published by Arthur Vorwald in the AMA *Archives of Industrial Health* in 1951. Evidence of the Q.A.M.A.'s involvement in this misrepresentation arises from co-conspirator Johns-Manville's membership of the Q.A.M.A., as well as correspondence from co-conspirators dated 10/29/47, 11/26/47, 3/6/48, 10/15/48, 3/8/49 and 9/6/50, and all indicating close monitoring of the editing process of Q.A.M.A.'s representative, Ivan Sabourin, acting on behalf of all Q.A.M.A. members.

(i) Defendants who were members of the Q.A.M.A. as described above, began on or about 1950, to formulate a plan to influence public opinion about the relationship between asbestos and cancer by influencing the medical literature on this subject and then touting and disseminating this literature to the public and to organizations and legislative bodies responsible for regulatory control of asbestos with the specific intent of misrepresenting the existing scientific information and suppressing contrary scientific data in their possession and control.

(j) This plan of misrepresentation and influence over the medical literature began on or about 1950 when the aforementioned Q.A.M.A. members selected Saranac Laboratories to do an evaluation of whether cancer was related to asbestos. After a preliminary report authored by Arthur Vorwald in 1952 indicated that a cancer/asbestos relationship might exist in experimental animals, these Q.A.M.A. members refused to further fund the study and it was terminated and never publicly discussed.

(k) As a result of the termination of this study, these defendants fraudulently withheld information from the public and affirmatively misrepresented to the public and responsible legislative and regulatory bodies that asbestos did not cause cancer, including affirmative misrepresentations by conspirators' agents K.W. Smith, M.D., Paul Cartier, M.D., A.J. Vorwald, M.D., A.J. Lanza, M.D., Vandiver Brown and Ivan Sabourin, said misrepresentations being directed to inter alia, U.S. government officials, Canadian government officials, U.S. National Cancer Institute, other medical organizations and the general public, including plaintiff.

(l) Subsequently, the Q.A.M.A. defendant conspirators contracted with the Industrial Hygiene Foundation and Dr. Daniel Braun to further study the relationship between asbestos exposure, asbestosis and lung cancer. In 1957, Drs.

Brown and Truan reported to the Q.A.M.A. that asbestosis did increase a worker's chances of incurring lung cancer.

(m) The Q.A.M.A. defendant conspirators/members thereafter caused, in 1958, a publication of the work of Braun and Truan in which the findings regarding increased incidence of cancer in persons with asbestosis was edited out by agents of the Q.A.M.A. The published version of this study contained a conclusion that asbestos exposure, alone, did not increase the incidence of lung cancer, a conclusion known by the defendant conspirators to be patently false.

(n) By falsifying and causing publication of studies concluding that asbestos exposure did not cause lung cancer and simultaneously omitting a documented finding that asbestosis did increase the risk of lung cancer, these Q.A.M.A. defendant conspirators affirmatively misrepresented to the public and concealed from the public the extent of risks associated with inhalation of asbestos fibers.

(o) In approximately 1958, these Q.A.M.A. defendant conspirators publicized the edited works of Drs. Braun and Truan at a symposium in an effort to fraudulently misrepresent to the public and persons exposed to asbestos that the inhalation of asbestos dust would not cause cancer.

(p) The fraudulent misrepresentations beginning in 1946, as elaborated above, and continuing with the publication of the 1958 Braun/Truan study influenced the standards set for threshold limit values for development of such standards to fail to lower the threshold limit value because of a cancer risk associated with asbestos inhalation.

(q) In 1967, Q.A.M.A. conspirators determined at their trade association meeting that they would intentionally mislead consumers about the extent of risks involved in inhalation of asbestos products.

(r) In 1952, a symposium regarding the health effects of asbestos was held at the Saranac Laboratories. The following conspirators were in attendance: Johns-Manville, Turner & Newall, Raybestos-Manhattan, and Q.A.M.A. members by way of their agents, Cartier, Sabourin and LaChance.

(s) At this meeting, the occurrence of lung cancer and asbestosis in product users was discussed and the carcinogenic properties of all fiber types of asbestos was also discussed. In an affirmative attempt to mislead the public about the extend of health risks associated with asbestos, and in an effort to fraudulently conceal those risks from the public, these defendants conspired to prevent publication of the record of this 1952 Saranac Symposium and it was not published. In addition, the conspirators induced Vorwald not to announce the results of his and Gardner's animal studies showing excess cancers in animals which thereby fraudulently misrepresented existing secret data which could not be publicized owing to the secrecy provisions contained in the 1936 Saranac Agreement heretofore described.

(t) The following conspirators were members of the trade organization known as the Asbestos Textile Institute (ATI): Raybestos-Manhattan, Johns-Manville, H. K. Porter, Keasby & Mattison, individually and through its alter-ego Turner & Newall and National Gypsum, Uniroyal, Inc., individually and through its alter-egos, CDU Holding Company, Uniroyal Holding Company and Uniroyal Goodrich Tire Company.

(u) In 1947, these conspirators, members of the ATI, received a report from W. C. L. Hemeon regarding asbestosis, which suggested re-evaluation of the then-existing threshold limit values for asbestos exposure. These defendants caused this report not to be published and thereby fraudulently concealed material facts about asbestos exposure from the public and affirmatively misrepresented to the public and class of persons exposed to asbestos that the existing threshold limit value was acceptable. Thereafter, these defendant conspirators withheld additional material information on the dust standards from the American Conference of Governmental Industrial Hygienists (ACGIH), thereby further influencing evaluations of threshold limit values for asbestos exposure.

(v) In 1953, conspirator National Gypsum through its agents, in response to an inquiry from the Indiana Division of Industrial Hygiene regarding health hazards of asbestos spray products, refused to mail a proposed response to that division indicating that respirators should be worn by applicators of the products. National Gypsum's response distorted and fraudulently misrepresented the need for applicators of asbestos spray products to wear respirators and fraudulently concealed from such applicators the need for respirators.

(w) In 1955, conspirator Johns-Manville, through its agent Kenneth Smith, caused to be published in the *AMA Archives of Industrial Health*, an article entitled "Pulmonary Disability in Asbestos Workers." This published study materially altered the results of an earlier study in 1949 concerning the same set of workers. This alteration of Dr. Smith's study constituted a fraudulent and material misrepresentation about the extent of the risk associated with asbestos inhalation.

(x) In 1955, the National Cancer Institute held a meeting at which conspirator Johns-Manville, individually and as an agent for other co-conspirators and A. Vorwald, as agent of co-conspirators, affirmatively misrepresented that there were no existing animal studies concerning the relationship between asbestos exposure and cancer, when, in fact, the conspirators were in secret possession of several studies which demonstrated that positive evidence did exist.

(y) In 1957, these conspirators, members of the ATI, jointly rejected a proposed research study on cancer and asbestos, which resulted in fraudulent concealment from the public of material facts regarding asbestos exposure and constituted an affirmative misrepresentation of the then-existing knowledge about asbestos exposure and lung cancer.

(z) In 1964, conspirators who were members of the ATI met to formulate a plan for rebutting the association between lung cancer and asbestos exposure that had been recently discussed by Dr. Irving J. Selikoff. Thereafter, these members of the ATI embarked upon a campaign to further misrepresent the association between asbestos exposure and lung cancer.

(aa) All conspirators identified above approved and ratified and furthered the previous conspiratorial acts of conspirators Johns-Manville, Raybestos Manhattan and A.J. Lanza, acting on behalf of Metropolitan Life Insurance Company, and all alleged co-conspirators during the dates and circumstances alleged above, acted as agents and co-conspirators for the other conspirators.

(bb) The Mellon Institute and the Industrial Hygiene Foundation (IHF) were research institutes whose functions included involvement in research regarding the health effects of inhaling asbestos dust.

(cc) Beginning in the early 1940s, the IHF was involved in a study by W.C.L. Hemeon entitled *Report of Preliminary Dust Investigation for Asbestos Textile Institute*, June 1947. This study was done in connection with members of the Asbestos Textile Institute (ATI). This study found that workers exposed to less than the recommended threshold limit value for asbestos were nonetheless developing disease. The IHF never published this study.

(dd) Beginning in the mid 1950's, the IHF and the Mellon Institute were involved in the publication of works by Drs. Braun and Truan entitled *An Epidemiological Study of Lung Cancer in Asbestos Miners*. In its original form in September, 1957, this study had concluded that workers with asbestosis had an increased incidence of lung cancer and that the Canadian government had been under-reporting cases of asbestosis. The final published version of this study in June, 1958, deleted the conclusion that workers with asbestosis suffered increased incidence of lung cancer and that the Canadian government had been under-reporting cases of asbestosis.

(ee) The IHF and the Mellon Institute conspired with the members of the Quebec Asbestos Mining Association (Q.A.M.A.) and their legal counsel, Ivan Sabourin, to delete the above-described information regarding asbestos and cancer.

(ff) The above-described actions of the IHF, the Mellon Institute, and Q.A.M.A. members constituted intentional deception and fraud in actively misleading the public about the extend of the hazards connected with breathing asbestos dust.

(gg) The above-described actions of the IHF and the Mellon Institute substantially contributed to retarding the development of knowledge about the hazards of asbestos and thereby substantially contributed to injuries suffered by the plaintiff.

20. The acts of the conspirators as described above, constitute a fraudulent concealment and/or a fraudulent misrepresentation which proximately caused injury to the plaintiff in the following manner:

94

(a) The material published or caused to be published by the IHF, the Mellon Institute, and Q.A.M.A. members was false and incomplete in that the defendants knowingly and deliberately deleted references to the known health hazards of asbestos and asbestos-related products.

(b) The IHF, the Mellon Institute, and Q.A.M.A. individually, as members of a conspiracy, and as agents of other co-conspirators, intended that the publication of false and misleading reports and/or the nondisclosure of documented reports of the health hazards of asbestos:

(1) maintain a favorable atmosphere for the continued sale and distribution of asbestos and asbestos-related products;

(2) assist in the continued pecuniary gain of the defendants through the sale of their products;

(3) influence in the defendants' favor proposed legislation to regulate asbestosexposure and;

(4) to provide a defense in lawsuits brought for injury resulting from asbestos disease.

(c) Plaintiff reasonably relied upon the published medical and scientific data documenting the purported safety of asbestos and asbestos-related products, and the absence of published medical and scientific reports on the hazards of asbestos and asbestos-related products to continue his exposure to asbestos because he believed it to be safe.

(d) Defendants individually, as members of a conspiracy, and as agents of other co-conspirators intended that the plaintiff rely upon the published reports regarding the safety of asbestos and asbestos-related products and upon the absence of published medical and scientific data regarding the hazards of asbestos and asbestos-related products, to continue his exposure to those products.

(e) Defendants individually, as members of a conspiracy, and as agents of other co-conspirators are in a position of superior knowledge regarding the health hazards of asbestos and therefore the plaintiff had a right to rely on the published reports commissioned by the defendants regarding the health hazards of asbestos and the absence of published medical and scientific data regarding the hazards of asbestos and asbestos-related products.

(f) Plaintiff suffered injury as a direct and proximate result of the acts alleged herein, and damages as described in the First Cause of Action.

FOURTH CAUSE OF ACTION— BREACH OF WARRANTY

21. The plaintiff incorporates by reference, as if fully set forth herein the allegations contained in paragraphs 1–20.

22. As manufacturers and distributors, the defendants warranted, expressly and impliedly, that their asbestos products were in a fit condition for their intended uses, which included activities such as those engaged in by the plaintiff during his working life, and that such products were of a merchantable quality.

23. The aforementioned defects and unreasonably dangerous conditions rendered the defendants' asbestos products unfit for the purpose for which they were intended to be used, thereby breaching the express and implied warranties that the defendants made to the plaintiff, which resulted in damages to the plaintiff as described in the First Cause of Action.

FIFTH CAUSE OF ACTION—AS TO DEFENDANT PPG ONLY—NEGLIGENCE

24. Plaintiff incorporates by reference as if fully set forth herein the allegations contained in paragraphs 1 through 23.

25. Defendant PPG Industries, Inc. (hereinafter "PPG") is the parent corporation of Pittsburgh-Corning Corporation, (hereinafter "subsidiary") a former manufacturer and marketer of asbestos-containing products.

26. Plaintiff was exposed to the asbestos-containing products manufactured by the subsidiary.

27. At all times relevant herein, PPG intervened on behalf of its subsidiary and researched the dangers and health consequences of asbestos exposure.

28. PPG and its subsidiary shared a common medical director who conducted the research on the hazards of asbestos exposure.

29. Through this undertaking, PPG created a duty to those, like plaintiff, who would come in contact with the asbestos contained in the products manufactured by its subsidiary.

30. PPG, upon assuming this duty and responsibility, failed to perform with reasonable care.

31. PPG created a dangerous, harmful and potentially deadly situation by not sharing its data on the dangers of asbestos exposure with those reasonably likely to be exposed, such as plaintiff.

32. PPG breached its duty to plaintiff by:

(a) failing to reasonably warn plaintiff of the hazards of asbestos exposure;

(b) failing to act reasonably with regard to the information it possessed concerning the hazards of exposure to asbestos;

(c) failing to provide plaintiff with the knowledge as to the possible precautions to protect against the harmful effects of asbestos exposure;

(d) failing to share its data on the dangers of asbestos exposure with those reasonably likely to be exposed, such as plaintiff;

(e) concealing the information it possessed about the hazards of asbestos from those reasonably likely to be exposed, such as plaintiff; and

(f) was otherwise negligent.

33. As a direct and proximate result of the negligence of defendant PPG Industries, Inc., plaintiff developed severe, permanent and disabling lung disease and suffered the damages and losses enumerated in the First Cause of Action.

SIXTH CAUSE OF ACTION—AS TO DEFENDANT PPG ONLY

RESTATEMENT OF TORTS SECTION 324a(A)

34. Plaintiff incorporates by reference as if fully set forth herein the allegations contained in paragraphs 1 through 33.

35. Defendant PPG undertook to render services for its subsidiary, including to perform research on the health effects of asbestos exposure.

36. PPG did or reasonably should have recognized this undertaking was necessary for the protection of third parties.

37. PPG breached this duty to third parties, such as plaintiff, by failing to exercise reasonable care to protect him from or warn him of the health hazards of asbestos exposure.

38. PPG'S failure to exercise reasonable care increased the risk of harm.

39. As a direct and proximate result of the negligence of defendant PPG Industries, Inc., plaintiff developed severe, permanent and disabling lung diseases and suffered the damages and losses enumerated in the First Cause of Action.

SEVENTH CAUSE OF ACTION—AS TO DEFENDANT PPG ONLY

RESTATEMENT OF TORTS SECTION 324A(b)

40. Plaintiff incorporates by reference as if fully set forth herein the allegations contained in paragraphs 1 through 39.

41. Defendant PPG's subsidiary owed a duty to plaintiff to reasonably research the health effects of asbestos exposure.

42. PPG undertook to perform this duty owed to plaintiff.

43. PPG breached this duty it undertook to perform for its subsidiary by:

(a) failing to reasonably warn plaintiff of the hazards of asbestos exposure;

(b) failing to act reasonably with regard to the information it possessed with regard to the hazards of exposure to asbestos;

(c) failing to provide plaintiff with the knowledge as to the possible precautions to protect against the harmful effects of asbestos exposure;

(d) failing to share its data on the dangers of asbestos exposure with those reasonably likely to be expose, such as plaintiff;

(e) concealing the information it possessed about the hazards of asbestos from those reasonably likely to be exposed, such as plaintiff; and

(f) was otherwise negligent.

EIGHTH CAUSE OF ACTION—AS TO DEFENDANT PPG ONLY

RESTATEMENT OF TORTS SECTION 324(c)

45. Plaintiff incorporates by reference as if fully set forth herein the allegations contained in paragraphs 1 through 44.

46. Plaintiff relied to his detriment on the undertaking of defendant PPG to research and warn him of the health hazards of asbestos exposure.

47. As a direct and proximate result of the negligence of defendant PPG Industries, Inc., plaintiff developed severe, permanent and disabling lung diseases and suffered the damages and losses enumerated in the First Cause of Action.

NINTH CAUSE OF ACTION—AS TO DEFENDANT PPG ONLY—NEGLIGENCE

48. Plaintiff incorporates by reference as if fully set forth herein the allegations contained in paragraphs 1 through 47.

49. Defendant PPG and its subsidiary, individually and in concert with each other and others, knowingly agreed and conspired among themselves to engage in a course of conduct that was reasonably likely to result in injury to the plaintiff.

50. PPG knew or should have known that the failure of its subsidiary to warn plaintiff of the harmful effects that asbestos exposure would cause plaintiff injury.

51. PPG gave substantial assistance and/or encouragement to its subsidiary in accomplishing the injury to the plaintiff.

52. As a direct and proximate result of the negligence of defendant PPG Industries, Inc., plaintiff developed severe, permanent and disabling lung diseases and suffered the damages and losses enumerated in the First Cause of Action.

TENTH CAUSE OF ACTION

53. Repeats and realleges each and every allegation contained in paragraphs 1 through 52.

54. At the time of the injured plaintiff's exposure to asbestos, plaintiff [*spouse's name*] was and still is the spouse of the injured plaintiff.

55. As a result of the negligence of each of the defendants, plaintiff [*spouse's name*] has lost the services, society, companionship, and consortium of the injured plaintiff.

WHEREFORE, the plaintiffs demand judgment against the defendants as follows:

(a) On the first, second, third, fourth, and tenth causes of action, against all defendants, jointly and severally, for damages in an amount deemed just and proper by the jury to adequately and fully compensate the plaintiffs for damages that they sustained, as well as punitive damages;

(b) On the fifth, sixth, seventh, eighth, and ninth causes of action, against defendant PPG Industries, Inc., jointly and severally, for damages in an amount deemed just and proper by the jury; to adequately and fully compensate the plaintiff for damages that he sustained, as well as punitive damages;

along with interest, the costs of suit herein, and whatever other and further relief that this Court deems just and proper.

Dated: [*date*]

Shapiro & Shapiro
1820 First Federal Plaza
Rochester, NY 14614
(716) 262-6350

SAMPLE INTERROGATORIES

SUPREME COURT OF THE STATE OF NEW YORK
EIGHTH JUDICIAL DISTRICT

In re EIGHTH JUDICIAL DISTRICT
ASBESTOS LITIGATION

> EIGHTH JUDICIAL
> DISTRICT ASBESTOS
> LITIGATION
> MASTER FILE

JOHN DOE and MARY DOE

Plaintiff(s)

VS

Defendants.

> PLAINTIFF'S ANSWERS
> TO DEFENDANTS'
> FIRST SET OF
> INTERROGATORIES
> AND REQUEST FOR
> PRODUCTION OF
> DOCUMENTS (revised)
>
> Index No.

Pursuant to Rule 3130 of the Civil Practice Law and Rules of New York State and Eighth Judicial District Asbestos Litigation Case Management Order, Number 1, defendants propound the following interrogatories to the plaintiffs, to be answered under oath and in accordance with the Civil Practice Law and Rules and said Case Management Order.

These interrogatories are continuing in nature and require you to file supplementary responses in accordance with the Civil Practice Law and Rules if you obtain further or different information after your initial responses and before trial, including in such supplemental responses, the date upon and the manner in which such further or different information came to your attention.

EXPLANATION AND DEFINITIONS

For the convenience of the plaintiffs and to prevent the need for duplicative answers, this document concurrently propounds interrogatories and request for production of documents. The documents to be produced are in each instance identified by responses to the interrogatories.

The terms used in these interrogatories and document requests and listed below are defined as follows:

A. "Decedent," "the decedent" or "your decedent" means the decedent and all persons acting on his or her behalf.

B. "Defendants," unless otherwise specified, means any defendant named as a party to this action as well as any predecessors in interest to any named defendants, and all other subsidiaries or divisions of any named defendants.

C. "Document" or "documents" means any writing of any kind, including originals and all nonidentical copies (whether different from the originals by reason of any notation made on such copies otherwise), as well as, without limitation, correspondence, memoranda, notes, calendars, diaries, statistics, letters, telegrams, minutes, contracts, reports, studies, checks, invoices, statements, receipts, returns, warranties, guarantees, summaries, pamphlets, books, prospectuses, intraoffice and interoffice communications, offers, notations of any sort of conversations, telephone calls, meetings or other communications, bulletins, magazines, publications, printed matter, photographs, motion pictures, video tapes, audio tapes, computer printouts, teletypes, telefaxes, invoices, work sheets, tapes, tape recordings, transcripts, graphic or audio records or representations of any kind, x-rays, and all drafts, alterations, modifications, changes and amendments to any of the foregoing, of which you have knowledge or which are now or were formerly in your actual or constructive possession, custody or control.

D. "He" means he and/or she; "him" means him and/or her; "his" means his and/or hers.

E. "Health Care Institution" means any entity providing health care services, including hospitals, laboratories, nursing homes, clinics and convalescent homes.

F. "Identify," "identity" and "identification"

    1. When used to refer to any entity other than a natural person, mean to state its full name, the present or last known address of its principal office or place of doing business and the type of entity (e.g., corporation, partnership, unincorporated association).

2. When used to refer to a natural person, mean to state the following:

   (a) The person's full name and present or last known home address, home telephone number, business address and business telephone number;

   (b) The person's present title and employer or other business affiliation;

   (c) The person's home address, home telephone number, business address and business telephone number at the time of the actions at which each interrogatory is directed; and

   (d) The person's employer and title at the time of the actions at which each interrogatory is directed.

3. When used to refer to a document, mean to state the following:

   (a) The subject of the document;

   (b) The title of the document;

   (c) The type of document (e.g., letter, memorandum, telegram, chart);

   (d) The date of the document, or, if the specific date thereof is unknown, the month and year or other best approximation of such date;

   (e) The identity of the person or persons who wrote, contributed to, prepared or originated such document; and

(f) The present or last known location and custodian of the document.

G. "Injured plaintiff" means a plaintiff who is asserting a claim for recovery of damages for his own personal injuries.

H. "Medical condition" means any condition or conditions for which a claim is being made, including any asbestos-related disease, any preexisting condition, or any condition brought about by an asbestos-related disease, including, but not limited to, physical or mental illness, disease, injury, symptom, complaint or adverse reaction.

I. "Person" means any natural person, firm, corporation, partnership, proprietorship, joint venture, organization, group of natural persons, or other association separately identifiable, whether or not such association or entity has a separate juristic existence in its own right

J. "Photograph" or "photographs" means any photographic prints, photographic slides, motion pictures or videotapes in your actual or constructive possession, custody or control.

K. "Physician" includes physicians, nurses, laboratory or other hospital personnel and other health care providers or practitioners of health care, including psychologists, social workers and counselors.

L. "Possession," "custody," or "control" includes the joint or several possession, custody or control not only by the person or persons to whom these interrogatories and requests are addressed, but also the joint or several possession, custody or control by each or any other person acting or purporting to act on behalf of the person, whether as employee, attorney, accountant, agent, sponsor, spokesperson or otherwise.

M. "Relates to" means supports, evidences, describes, mentions, refers to, contradicts or comprises.

INSTRUCTIONS

A. In the event that an action involves two named plaintiffs and each plaintiff is asserting a claim for recovery of damages for his own personal injuries, a separate set of responses to these interrogatories and document request should be served for each plaintiff.

B. In the event that an action is sued by a representative of a decedent's estate and that representative is asserting a claim for recovery of damages for his own personal injuries, separate sets of responses to these interrogatories and document requests should be served for the decedent and for the representative of decedent's estate.

C. With respect to each interrogatory, in addition to supplying the information asked for and identifying the specific documents referred to, identify all documents which were referred to in preparing the answer thereof.

D. If any document identified in an answer to an interrogatory was, but is no longer, in your possession or subject to your custody or control, or was known to you, but is no longer in existence, state what disposition was made of it or what became of it.

E. If any document is withheld from production hereunder on the basis of a claim of privilege or otherwise, identify each such document and the grounds upon which its production is being withheld.

F. The following releases and authorizations should be signed by the plaintiff or a person with proper authority and returned with the responses to these interrogatories:

1. A release in the form annexed hereto as Exhibit A for defendants to obtain a record of injured plaintiff's/decedent's tax records from the Internal Revenue Service and employment and earnings history from the Social Security Administration;

2. A release in the form annexed hereto as Exhibit B for each workers' compensation claim file referred to in the responses to these interrogatories;

3. Authorizations in the form annexed hereto as Exhibit C to obtain injured plaintiff's/decedent's employment records from each employer identified or referred to in the responses to these interrogatories;

4. Medical records authorizations in the form annexed hereto as Exhibit D to obtain injured plaintiff's/decedent's medical records from each physician, health care institution, and pharmacy identified or referred to in the responses to these interrogatories.

5. If applicable, a release in the form annexed as Exhibit E to obtain injured plaintiff's/decedent's military service records; and

6. A release in the form annexed as Exhibit F to obtain injured plaintiff's/ decedent's school records.

G. You are requested to furnish all information in your possession and all information available to you, not merely such information as you know of your own personal knowledge but also all knowledge that is available to you, your representatives, attorneys and agents, by reason of inquiry, including inquiry of their representatives. Where a response to the following interrogatories sets forth information that is not based upon your own personal knowledge, but rather upon the knowledge of your representatives, attorneys and agents, you should so indicate in your response to that interrogatory.

INTERROGATORIES

A. PERSONAL BACKGROUND OF PLAINTIFF AS REPRESENTATIVE OF DECEDENT'S ESTATE:

1. If you represent decedent's estate, state the following for yourself:

    (a) Full name and all other names by which you have been known;

    (b) Relationship to the decedent;

    (c) Date and place of birth;

    (d) Address;

    (e) Social Security number;

(f) Present marital status and, if applicable, name of present spouse and date of marriage; and

(g) Dates of all prior marriages, spouses' names, and dates of termination of marriages.

B. PERSONAL BACKGROUND OF INJURED PLAINTIFF/DECEDENT:

2. State the following for injured plaintiff/decedent:

(a) Full name and all other names by which injured plaintiff/decedent has been known;

(b) Date and place of birth;

(c) Whether injured plaintiff/decedent was an adopted child and, if adopted, state date of adoption;

(d) Present age; or date and place of death;

(e) Present marital status and, if applicable, name of present spouse and date of marriage, or marital status at the time of death, and if applicable, the name of spouse at the time of death and date of marriage;

(f) Dates of all prior marriages, spouses' names, and dates of termination of marriages;

(g) Present home address, or home address at time of death; and

(h) Social Security number.

3. State the following with regard to injured plaintiff's/decedent's father, mother, and each sibling:

(a) Name, relationship and date of birth;

(b) Current address (if deceased, state last known address);

(c) Current condition of each one's health, including any specific medical problems;

(d) If either of injured plaintiff's/decedent's parents is deceased, please state for each deceased parent:

(i) Specific medical problems;

(ii) Date and place of death;

(iii) Cause of death.

(e) If injured plaintiff's/decedent's grandparent, aunt, uncle, great aunt, great uncle or first cousin has had any respiratory illness (other than common colds), cardiac problem, or any cancer, state as to each:

(i) Name, relationship and date of birth;

(ii) Current address (if deceased, state last known address); and

(iii) The specific respiratory illness, cardiac problem, or cancer the individual had or has.

4. State the following with regard to each of injured plaintiff's/decedent's children:

(a) Name;

(b) Date of birth;

(c) Sex;

(d) Current address (if deceased, state the last known address);

(e) Whether natural child or adopted child and, if adopted, state date of adoption;

(f) Current state of health, including a statement of specific medical problems;

(g) If any of injured plaintiff's/decedent's children are deceased, state for each deceased child:

    (i) Specific medical problems;

    (ii) Date and place of death; and

    (iii) Cause of death.

5. List all injured plaintiff's/decedent's residences, the date injured plaintiff/decedent resided at each, and with respect to each state:

(a) Whether such residence contained asbestos insulation;

(b) Whether any improvements were made to the residence (i.e., insulation, rewiring, etc.);

(c) The type of fuel used for heating;

(d) The type of fuel used for cooking; and

(e) Whether injured plaintiff/decedent ever changed residence for health reasons and, if so, the residence left and the health reason for leaving.

6. Identify each member of the injured plaintiff's/decedent's household in the last five years, or during the last five years prior to death, and also state as to each:

   (a) His age, occupation, and relationship to the injured plaintiff/decedent; and

   (b) The portion of the last 12 months, or the last 12 months of the decedent's life, during which he was a member of the household.

7. List injured plaintiff's/decedent's hobbies or the major leisure activities in which he engaged during the last twenty years, or the last twenty years of his life. If the injured plaintiff/decedent did not have hobbies or participate in leisure activities, describe how he spent his leisure time

8. Did injured plaintiff/decedent or his spouse ever file for divorce against the other?

   If your answer is yes, state the date of suit, its disposition, and the date of disposition.

9. Were injured plaintiff/decedent and his spouse ever separated for any period more than 48 hours because of a marital disagreement?

   If your answer is yes, indicate every such incident, stating the reason for the separation and the length of time of each separation.

10. Was injured plaintiff/decedent every a party to or a witness in any lawsuit, court or administrative proceeding?

If your answer is yes, state:

(a) Whether injured plaintiff/decedent was a party or a witness and, if a party, whether he was a plaintiff or a defendant;

(b) The title of the lawsuit or proceeding, the court or agency in which it was brought, and the docket number;

(c) The nature of the charges or claims and, if injured plaintiff/decedent was a witness, the substance of his testimony;

(d) The disposition of the case; and

(e) Identify all insurance carriers or administrative agencies that either made payment or declined to make payment with respect to each such lawsuit or claim.

11. Has injured plaintiff/decedent ever applied and been rejected for a life insurance, medical insurance, or disability insurance policy?

If your answer is yes, state with regard to each such event:

(a) The identity of the insurer to whom such application was made;

(b) The date of such application;

(c) The identity of any physician conducting a physical examination with regard to such application and the date thereof;

(d) The reason for such rejection; and

(e) Produce all documentation of said application and rejection.

C. EMPLOYMENT HISTORY

12. Have you or anyone on your behalf requested from the Social Security Administration a listing of all of the injured plaintiff's/decedent's employers and dates of employment?

If your answer is yes, attach a copy of such listing to your responses to these interrogatories.

If not available, execute and provide a release in the form annexed as Exhibit A.

13. Identify each and every employer that injured plaintiff/decedent had from the time he was first employed to the present, or to the time of his death, including any and all military service, and as to each, state:

(a) The period of time injured plaintiff/decedent worked for each such employer;

(b) Each position/job title which injured plaintiff/decedent held with each such employer and the dates each such position/job title was held by injured plaintiff/decedent;

(c) The nature of the work performed;

(d) The location(s) of injured plaintiff's/decedent's particular jobsite(s);

(e) The nature of the materials or products injured plaintiff/decedent worked with; and

(f) Whether said activity involved working in the presence of dust, pollutants, or toxic substances and, if so:

    (i) Identify by name or type said dust, pollutants, or toxic substances;

    (ii) State whether any suction device, fan, or other ventilation system was present at the jobsite; and

    (iii) State whether the employer or any governmental agency or union took air samplings at the jobsite and, if so, identify the persons who took the air samplings, the dates such samplings were taken and the persons presently having possession or control of any documents relating to such air samplings.

14. If injured plaintiff/decedent was self-employed at any time, identify each such business, and as to each, state:

(a) The period during which injured plaintiff/decedent was self-employed;

(b) The nature of the work performed;

(c) The location(s) of injured plaintiff's/decedent's particular jobsite(s);

(d) The nature of the materials or products injured plaintiff/decedent worked with; and

(e) Whether said activity involved working in the present of dust, pollutants, or toxic substances and, if so:

  (i) Identify by name or type said dust, pollutants, or toxic substances;

  (ii) State whether any suction device, fan, or other ventilation system was present at the jobsite; and

  (iii) State whether the employer, any governmental agency, any union or any other person took air samplings at any jobsite at which injured plaintiff/decedent worked, and, if so, identify the person(s) who took the air samples, the dates such air samples were taken and the persons presently having possession or control of any documents relating to such air samples.

15. Did injuries plaintiff/decedent ever lose a job, change jobs or change his position with an employer for health reasons?

If your answer is yes, state as to each such event:

(a) The employer and job position which injured plaintiff/decedent left:

(b) The date of such event;

(c) The health reason for such event; and

    (d) The new employer and/or job position which injured plaintiff/decedent next assumed.

16. Are you aware of, have you ever seen, or do you or any attorney possess or have access to any photographs, charts, drawings, diagrams or other graphic representations depicting work conditions at work sites where you claim injured plaintiff/decedent was exposed to asbestos materials and/or asbestos-containing products?

If your answer is yes, with respect to each:

    (a) Identify each such photograph or other document, including a statement as to which views, scenes or objects it purports to depict, the person who took or prepared each such photograph or other document, and the date taken or prepared;

    (b) State whether the photograph or other document was prepared on your behalf or on behalf of other persons allegedly exposed to asbestos or as a result of circumstances relating to this or any other lawsuit; and

    (c) Attach a copy.

17. During the period of time for which you claim injured plaintiff/decedent was exposed to asbestos materials and/or asbestos-containing products, did injured plaintiff/decedent share a household with any other person(s) who worked or was employed outside the household?

If your answer is yes, identify:

(a) Each such other person;

(b) The period(s) of time each such other person shared such household;

(c) The period(s) of time each such other person worked or was so employed;

(d) The nature of each job held or job title for each such other person in each such period of time; and

(e) Each and every employer of each such other person in each such period of time.

D. TOXIC EXPOSURES

18. Was injured plaintiff/decedent ever exposed to or did injured plaintiff/decedent ever use, inhale or ingest any of the following substances on a regular basis or at work?

    If your answer is yes, state the date(s), place(s), and circumstances thereof:

    (a) Acids;

    (b) Aluminum;

    (c) Ammonia;

    (d) Arsenic;

    (e) Barium;

    (f) Berylium;

    (g) Butanol;

    (h) Cadmium;

(i) Carborundum;

(j) Chloroethylene;

(k) Chlorine;

(l) Chromate;

(m) Chromite;

(n) Chromium;

(o) Coal and/or coal dust

(p) Coal tar;

(q) Cotton dust;

(r) Creosote;

(s) Epoxy;

(t) Ethanol;

(u) Formaldehyde;

(v) Grinding dust;

(w) Iron;

(x) Isocyanates;

(y) Isopropanol;

(z) Lead;

(aa) Live chickens;

(bb) Manganese;

(cc) Nickel;

(dd) Nitrogen dioxide;

(ee) Nuclear radiation;

(ff) Ozone;

(gg) Petroleum distillates;

(hh) Phosgene;

(ii) Radiation;

(jj) Silica;

(kk) Titanium;

(ll) Toluene;

(mm) Welding smoke or fumes;

(nn) Zylene; or

(oo) Zinc.

19. From the time of his birth to the present or to the time of his death, did injured plaintiff/decedent ever use cigarettes, cigars, pipes, smokeless tobacco, or any other tobacco substance?

If your answer is yes, state the following:

(a) The brand and type of tobacco product(s) used (e.g., filter, non-filter, chewing tobacco);

(b) The period(s) during which he used each such product;

(c) The amount of the product used per day, during each period of time (e.g., two packs of cigarettes per day for two years);

(d) Whether injured plaintiff/decedent was ever told that he was suffering from any disease or illness contributed to or caused by use of tobacco, and if so identify each person who gave injured plaintiff/decedent any such advice, the dates on which the advice was given, and state exactly what, if anything, injured plaintiff/decedent did in response to that advice;

(e) Whether the injured plaintiff/decedent was ever advised that use of tobacco products could adversely affect his health, and if so, identify each person who gave injured plaintiff/decedent any such advice, the dates on which the advice was given, and state exactly what, if anything, injured plaintiff/decedent did in response to that advice; and

(f) Whether injured plaintiff/decedent was ever advised to stop using tobacco products, and if so, identify each person who gave injured plaintiff/decedent any such advice, the dates on which the advice was given, and state exactly what, if anything, injured plaintiff/decedent did in response to that advice.

20. For each spouse and member of injured plaintiff's/decedent's household, from injured plaintiff's/decedent's birth until the present or until his death, state whether each individual ever used cigarettes, cigars, pipes, smokeless tobacco, or any other tobacco substance, and if so, state the following for each:

(a) The brand and type of tobacco product(s) used (e.g., filter, non-filter, chewing tobacco);

(b) The period(s) during which he used each such product; and

(c) Whether he was ever told by a doctor that he is or was suffering from any disease or illness caused or contributed to by his use of tobacco, and if so, when and by whom.

21. If injured plaintiff/decedent ever worked in an office or other enclosed space, state whether injured plaintiff/decedent shared a room with anyone who used or smoked cigarettes, cigars or pipes.

22. Did injured plaintiff/decedent consume alcoholic beverages?

If your answer is yes, state the following:

(a) The type of alcoholic beverages consumed;

(b) The periods during which injured plaintiff/decedent consumed each such alcoholic beverage;

(c) The amount of such beverage injured plaintiff/decedent consumed each day during each period of use; and

(d) Whether injured plaintiff/decedent was ever treated for any illness or disease related to his consumption of alcoholic beverages or was ever advised to reduce his consumption.

23. Did injured plaintiff/decedent ever take any pre-scription medication, any non-prescription medication, or any other drugs for the treatment of respiratory problems, cardiac problems, gastrointestinal problems, cancer or any chronic health condition or illness?

If your answer is yes, state for each:

(a) The medication or drug taken;

(b) The amount of medication or drug taken and the period over which it was taken;

(c) The reason for taking the medication or drug; and

(d) If the medication was prescribed:

(i) Identify the person prescribing the medication;

(ii) Identify the pharmacy filling the pre-scription; and

(iii) Produce any document reflecting the prescribing, filling, or payment of any prescription medication.

E. PRODUCT INFORMATION

24. State with regard to each asbestos material and/or asbestos-containing product to which injured plaintiff/decedent allegedly has every been exposed, or which the injured plaintiff/decedent allegedly has ever used, ingested or inhaled:

(a) The kind or type of material or product, using its generic name (e.g., asbestos block, asbestos cement, asbestos cloth, brake linings);

(b) The trade name, brand name and trades symbol;

(c) The name of the manufacturer, distributor(s), and miner(s) of such material or product;

(d) The color, dimensions, shape, form, texture, weight, appearance and flexibility of each material or product; (e)

The appearance of the package or container, indicating the manner of packaging, size, dimensions, color and weight;

(f) The name, logo, label, numerical and alphabetical markings and other markings or words, including warnings, on the material product, package and/or container;

(g) The dates of injured plaintiff's/decedent's exposure to each material or product;

(h) The exact location(s) at which injured plaintiff/decedent was working, indicating each jobsite, ship, building and place where injured plaintiff/decedent was exposed to, used, ingested or inhaled each material or product, and for each:

(i) State the date of the exposure;

(ii) Identify injured plaintiff's/decedent's employer at the time of exposure; and

(iii) Describe injured plaintiff's/decedent's activities and duties at the time of exposure.

(i) Whether or not you contend that exposure to such material or product caused injured plaintiff's/decedent's injuries or damages;

(j) The identity of all sources of information stated in response to subparts (a) through (i) (including your personal knowledge, witnesses and documents); and for each source state the material and/or product identified and the factual basis of the identification.

25. If you contend that injured plaintiff/decedent was exposed to, used, ingested or inhaled asbestos materials and/or asbestos-containing products at any time other than in the scope of his employment, state for each such exposure:

(a) The date, location and circumstances;

(b) The type of material or product, using its generic name (e.g., asbestos block, asbestos cement, asbestos cloth, brake linings);

(c) The trade name, brand name and trade symbol;

(d) The name of the manufacturer, distributors, and miners of such material or product;

(e) The color, dimensions, shape, form, texture, weight, appearance and flexibility of each material or product;

(f) The appearance of the package or container, indicating the manner of packaging, size, dimensions, color and weight;

(g) The name, logo, label, numerical and alphabetical markings and other markings or words, including warnings, on the material, product, package and/or container; and

(h) The identity of all sources of information stated in response to subparts (a) through (g) (including your personal knowledge, witnesses and documents); and for each source state the material or product identified and the factual basis of the identification.

26. Are you aware of, or have you ever seen, or do you possess or have access to any photographs of asbestos materials or asbestos-containing products or any cartons, containers, labels or wrappers of any asbestos materials or asbestos-containing products which you claim injured plaintiff/decedent actually applied or was exposed to?

If your answer is yes, state:

(a) The identity of each such photograph or other document, including a statement as to which objects its purports to depict, the person who took or prepared each such photograph or other document, and the date taken or prepared;

(b) Whether each such photograph or other document was prepared on your behalf or on behalf of other persons allegedly exposed to asbestos or as a result of circumstances relating to this or any other lawsuit; and

(c) Attach a copy.

26A. Have you or has injured plaintiff/decedent over identified an asbestos material or asbestos-containing product or any cartons, containers, labels or wrappers of any asbestos materials or asbestos-containing products which you claim injured plaintiff/decedent actually applied or was exposed to from a photograph displayed to you or injured plaintiff/decedent by your attorney?

If your answer is yes, state:

(a) The identity of each such photograph or other document, including a statement as to which objects it purports to depict, the person who took or prepared each such photograph or other document, and the date taken or prepared;

(b) Whether each such photograph or other document was prepared on your behalf or on behalf of other persons allegedly exposed to asbestos or as a result of circumstances relating to this or any other lawsuit; and

(c) Attach a copy.

27. Other than those persons identified in your answers to interrogatories 24 through 26, identify anyone with knowledge of asbestos products to which injured plaintiff/decedent may have been exposed, and as to each such person:

(a) Identify the person's employer at the time of the alleged asbestos exposure;

(b) State the nature of the person's work;

(c) Identify the particular jobsite(s) where the person worked; and

(d) State the person's dates of employment.

28. Identify by date, vendee (e.g., Government Services Administration, United States Navy, Brooklyn Navy Shipyard or private entity or individual), vendee representative, and vendor representative, if any, all invoices, bills, statements, and any other writings or records which you contend evidence the sale of any products containing asbestos to any of the places of employment at which you claim that injured plaintiff/decedent was exposed to asbestos. In addition, identify the present custodian of each item.

F. CLAIMS AGAINST DEFENDANTS

29. State separately as to each defendant:

(a) Each and every alleged act or omission constituting negligence;

(b) The identity of all persons allegedly acting or omitting to act on behalf of the defendant;

(c) How and in what manner such act or omission caused or contributed to injured plaintiff's/decedent's injury.

30. If you contend that the inhalation of asbestos dust and/or asbestos-containing particles is highly dangerous and the proximate cause of any disease, state:

    (a) The disease allegedly caused;

    (b) The basis for the contention; and

    (c) The date(s) on which it allegedly became well established or well known that the inhalation of asbestos dust and/or asbestos-containing particles is highly dangerous and the proximate cause of the diseases listed in response to subpart (a).

31. If you contend that any defendant violated or was negligent in following any trade standards, safety standards, statutes, rules, regulations or ordinances for the mining, design, production, or manufacturing process or use for asbestos or any asbestos-containing product, identify such defendants and state with respect to each defendant:

    (a) The name and citation of each standard, statute, rule, or regulation which you contend the defendant violated and the date of each such violation; and

    (b) The manner in which the defendant violated or was negligent in following the standard, statute, rule, or regulation described in subpart (a) of this interrogatory.

32. If you contend that any defendant knew or should have known that the asbestos present in asbestos-containing products allegedly mined,

manufactured, distributed and/or sold by such defendant was inherently dangerous, defective, ultra-hazardous, unsound for use, or otherwise harmful, identify such defendants and with respect to each defendant:

(a) Identify the persons acting on its behalf who allegedly had actual knowledge that the asbestos contained in any product of such defendant was inherently dangerous, defective, ultra-hazardous, unsound for use or otherwise harmful;

(b) State the substance and date of the actual knowledge possessed by each person identified in subpart (a) above;

(c) Identify all documents which support each contention, giving a summary of the substantive contents of each or, alternatively, attach such documents hereto; and

(d) State the complete factual basis for any contention that such defendant should have known of the alleged dangers of asbestos or asbestos-containing products.

33. If you contend that any defendant failed to properly warn or instruct injured plaintiff/decedent as to the dangers of asbestos or asbestos-containing products, identify such defendants and with respect to each defendant:

(a) Identify the product(s); and

(b) Describe the exact danger or hazardous condition or use of said product(s) about which you contend such defendant should have warned or instructed injured plaintiff/decedent.

34. If you contend that any defendant's negligence consisted of the use of an improper or unsuitable design for asbestos or asbestos-containing products, identify such defendants and with respect to each defendant describe how its design was improper or unsuitable for the product.

35. If you contend that injured plaintiff's/decedent's medical condition(s) was due to any defendant's negligence in the mining, manufacture or assembly of any asbestos and/or asbestos-containing product, identify each such defendant and each such asbestos and/or asbestos-containing product and with respect to each defendant and each product:

   (a) State each act which such defendant did or failed to do in the manufacture or assembly of such product which caused or contributed to injured plaintiff's/decedent's medical condition(s);

   (b) Describe the defect or defective condition in the product which you contend was caused by such defendant's conduct as described in subpart (a) of this interrogatory; and

   (c) Describe what you contend such defendant should have done, or should have refrained from doing, in the mining, manufacture or assembly of the product.

36. If you contend that injured plaintiff's/decedent's injuries or damages were in any way due to any

defendant's negligence in the testing or inspection of asbestos or any asbestos-containing product, identify each such defendant and each such asbestos and/or asbestos-containing product and with respect to each defendant and each product:

(a) State each act which such defendant did or failed to do in the testing or inspecting of the product which caused injured plaintiff's/decedent's medical condition(s);

(b) Describe the defect or defective condition in the product which you contend was caused by such defendant's conduct as described in subpart (a) of this interrogatory; and

(c) Describe what you contend such defendant should have done, or should have refrained from doing, in the testing or inspection of the product.

37. If you contend that any defendant stated, advertised, or otherwise represented to injured plaintiff/decedent or to any other purchaser or user that there were no health hazards associated with asbestos and/or asbestos-containing products, identify each such defendant and with respect to each defendant state:

(a) The content of each such statement, advertisement or representation;

(b) The date, place and manner of such acts;

(c) All facts which support each such contention; and

(d) The identity of all persons involved in such contentions.

38. If you contend that asbestos or any asbestos-containing product failed to satisfy any express warranty or other representation of any defendant concerning potential uses or standards of performance, or that asbestos or any asbestos-containing product was unfit for its intended use, identify each such product and defendant and with respect to each product and defendant:

(a) State the content and source of all representations or warranties which allegedly were not fulfilled;

(b) State all the facts which you contend prove the existence of the warranties or representations as described in subpart (a);

(c) Describe the manner in which the product did not conform to the above-described warranties or representations;

(d) State the date(s) on which injured plaintiff/decedent gave notice of said breach(es) of warranty or misrepresentation(s);

(e) State to whom and in what manner injured plaintiff/decedent gave notice of said breach(es) of warranty or misrepresentation(s);

(f) State how long after injured plaintiff/decedent was exposed to, used, ingested or inhaled the product did injured plaintiff/decedent give notice of said breach(es) of warranty or misrepresentation(s); and

(g) If injured plaintiff/decedent did not give notice of said breach(es) of warranty or misrepresentation(s), state why said notice was not given, whether you contend that each defendant was not prejudiced by lack of notice or lack of timely notice, and the facts upon which you rely in support of that contention.

39. If you contend that asbestos or any asbestos-containing product failed to satisfy any implied warranty or other representation of any defendant concerning potential uses or standards of performance, or that asbestos or any asbestos-containing product was unfit for its intended use, identify each such product and defendant and with respect to each product and defendant:

(a) Describe the manner in which the product did not conform to the above-described warranties or representations;

(b) Explain how injured plaintiff/decedent relied upon the warranties or representations; and

(c) State in what manner each defendant's breach of any or all warranties or misrepresentations as alleged contributed to or caused injured plaintiff's/decedent's injuries or damages, giving full details as to how the proper fitness or quality of the product would have prevented injured plaintiff's/decedent's injuries or damages.

40. If you contend that asbestos or any asbestos-containing product was inherently dangerous when put into normal or foreseeable use or operation, identify each such product and defendant and describe the alleged inherent danger or hazard in the product.

41. If you contend that any defendant conspired to deprive the public, injured plaintiff/decedent and others similarly situated of relevant medical and scientific data, or actively defrauded the public, injured plaintiff/decedent and others similarly situated, by the solicitation of favorable scientific and medical data, or otherwise, identify each defendant against whom such claim is made and state:

    (a) The date, place and manner of such acts;

    (b) The medical and scientific data of which the public was deprived or which was solicited;

    (c) All facts which support each such contention; and

    (d) The identity of all persons involved in such contentions.

42. If you contend that any defendant acted in concert to deprive injured plaintiff/decedent, the public and others similarly situated, or to actively defraud injured plaintiff/decedent, the public and others similarly situated, identify each defendant against whom such claim is made and state:

    (a) The date, place and manner of such acts;

(b) All facts which support each such contention; and

(c) The identity of all persons involved in such contentions.

43. If you contend that intentional conduct of any defendant is actionable, identify each such defendant and with respect to each defendant state:

(a) The intentional conduct;

(b) The date, place and manner of such acts;

(c) All facts which support such contention;

and

(d) The identity of all persons involved in such contentions.

44. If you contend that any defendant intentionally suppressed and/or concealed by affirmative act material facts as to health hazards associated with the purchase of, use of, and/or exposure to asbestos or any asbestos-containing product, identify each such defendant and state as to each:

(a) The date, place and manner of such affirmative acts;

(b) The material facts suppressed or concealed;

(c) All facts which support each such contention; and

(d) The identity of all persons involved in such acts.

45. If you are asserting claims based upon market share or percentage of injured plaintiff's/decedent's total alleged contact or exposure to asbestos or materials containing asbestos:

    (a) State the market share or percentage which you attribute to each individual or entity which you claim was a manufacturer or supplier of asbestos or materials containing asbestos;

    (b) Indicate or identify:

        (i) The manner of and the factors relied upon in making each such percentage calculation;

        (ii) The individuals assisting you or otherwise involved in calculating the above percentages;

        (iii) All documents, writings or other records, if any, relied upon in your calculation and the present location and identity of the present custodian of each such document, writing or other records; and

    (c) If you are unable to attribute such percentages, state all efforts you have made to ascertain such percentages.

46. If you contend that you are entitled to punitive damages against any defendant, identify each such defendant and with respect to each defendant, identify each such defendant and with respect to defendant state the basis for this contention.

G. WARNING AND SAFETY PRACTICES

47. List all publications which injured plaintiff/decedent regularly received or read.

48. Did injured plaintiff/decedent regularly receive or read "The Asbestos Worker"?

49. Did injured plaintiff/decedent at any time receive or learn about any advice, publication, warning, order, directive, requirement, or recommendation, whether written or oral, which advised or warned of the possible harmful effects of exposure to, or inhalation of, asbestos, or asbestos-containing products?

    If your answer is yes, state:

    (a) The nature and exact wording of such advice, warning, recommendation, etc.;

    (b) The identity of each source of such advice, warning, recommendation, etc.;

    (c) The date, time, place, manner and circumstances when each such advice, warning, recommendation, etc., was given; and

    (d) The identity of each witness to decedent's receipt of such advice, warning, recommendation, etc.

50. Was injured plaintiff/decedent ever a member of any labor union?

    If your answer is yes, state:

    (a) The identity of each local, national and international union;

140

(b) The inclusive dates of injured plaintiff's/decedent's membership; and

(c) Any position(s) injured plaintiff/decedent held with each such union, and the dates during which he held such positions.

51. Did injured plaintiff/decedent receive any newspapers, newsletters, or other publications from any labor union?

If your answer is yes, state whether such publications ever discussed the subject of worker exposure to asbestos, and if so:

(a) Identify the publication; and

(b) State the date(s) that such publication discussed the subject of asbestos and the nature of said discussion.

52. Did injured plaintiff/decedent ever attend any international, national, regional or local union meetings, seminars, conferences, or conventions where the subject of occupational health, and, in particular, exposure to asbestos, was discussed?

If your answer is yes:

(a) Identify such meeting, seminar, conference or convention and state the date(s) and place held;

(b) State the reason and/or official capacity for injured plaintiff/decedent attending;

(c) Identify the speaker(s);

(d) Summarize the information presented concerning exposure to asbestos; and

(e) Identify any persons with whom injured plaintiff/decedent discussed the information presented.

53. Was injured plaintiff/decedent ever informed by any employer or by any person in an official capacity in his local or international union of any possible hazards associated with exposure to asbestos dust or fiber?

If your answer is yes, state:

(a) The identity and official capacity of the individual or individuals who furnished injured plaintiff/decedent with such information;

(b) The date and place such information was furnished;

(c) The manner in which such information was communicated;

(d) The nature of such information; and

(e) What action, if any, injured plaintiff/decedent took in response to such information.

54. Did injured plaintiff/decedent ever see any warning labels on packages or containers of asbestos products?

If your answer is yes, state:

(a) The type of product using its generic name;

(b) The trade name, brand name and trade symbol;

(c) The name of the manufacturer, distributors and miners of such product;

(d) The appearance of the package or container, indicating the manner of packaging, size, dimensions, color and weight;

(e) The name, logo, label, numerical and alphabetical markings or words on the package or container;

(f) When and where injured plaintiff/decedent saw the labels; and

(g) The nature of the warnings.

55. Did injured plaintiff/decedent ever see or receive any information, instruction, direction, warning, or directive, from any source whatsoever, concerning alleged dangers of exposure to asbestos materials or asbestos-containing products?

If your answer is yes, identify:

(a) Each such warning, directive, notification, direction, instruction, or information;

(b) The means by which such was given to injured plaintiff/decedent;

(c) The source and the date on which it was received by injured plaintiff/decedent; and

(d) Injured plaintiff's/decedent's response or reaction, including any complaints made or changes in work habits.

56. Did injured plaintiff/decedent have available for use during any period of his employment, respirators or masks or other dust inhalation inhibitor or protective gear?

If your answer is yes, state:

(a) The period of time during which said items were available;

(b) What instructions were given with regard to the use of each of said items;

(c) Whether injured plaintiff/decedent used said items and the dates of his use;

(d) What percentage of time during which injured plaintiff/decedent was exposed to asbestos materials or asbestos-containing products, injured plaintiff/decedent used said items; and

(e) Whether injured plaintiff/decedent ever requested said items, and if so, when, where and to whom the request was made, and the response to the request.

57. Did anyone, at any time, suggest, recommend or require that injured plaintiff/decedent use a respirator or mask or other dust inhalation inhibitor or protective gear when he used or was exposed to asbestos materials or asbestos-containing products or dust?

If your answer is yes, state:

(a) The identity of the person or entity making such suggestion, recommendation or requirement;

(b) The date on which each such suggestion, recommendation or requirement was made;

(c) The substance of each such suggestion, recommendation or requirement; and

(d) What action, if any, injured plaintiff/decedent took in response to each suggestion, recommendation or requirement.

H. MEDICAL INFORMATION

58. For every physician by whom injured plaintiff/decedent has ever been treated or examined or with whom injured plaintiff/decedent consulted, state the following:

(a) The identity of the physician;

(b) Dates of treatment, examination or consultation; and

(c) The nature of such treatment, examination or consultation.

59. For every health care institution in which injured plaintiff/decedent has ever been admitted, treated, tested or examined, whether as an in-patient or as an out-patient, state:

(a) The identity of the health care institution;

(b) The date of and nature of each admission, treatment, test or examination; and

(c) The diagnosis at each admission, treatment, test or examination.

60. For each and every medical condition which you contend is directly or indirectly related to injured

plaintiff's/decedent's exposure to asbestos or asbestos-containing products, state:

(a) The nature and description of such medical condition;

(b) The disease, disability or physical condition to which said medical condition is related and the nature and extent of such relationship;

(c) The date on which injured plaintiff/decedent first exhibited signs of the medical condition;

(d) The date upon which each medical condition was first reported to a physician;

(e) The identity of each physician to whom said medical condition was reported;

(f) Any physical change in injured plaintiff's/decedent's appearance occasioned by such medical condition;

(g) Each part of injured plaintiff's/decedent's body which you contend had been thus affected;

(h) Whether you claim that such medical condition caused injured plaintiff/decedent to suffer a disability and, if so, when injured plaintiff/decedent first suffered such a disability; and

(i) The date each such medical condition ceased to affect injured plaintiff/decedent.

61. State the date that injured plaintiff/decedent first noticed, if ever, each of the following symptoms or complaints:

    (a) Shortness of breath;

    (b) Crackling noises in the lungs;

    (c) Coughing;

    (d) Clubbing or swelling of the fingers;

    (e) Discoloration of the skin;

    (f) Wheezing;

    (g) Chest pain;

    (h) Abdominal swelling;

    (i) Weight loss;

    (j) Respiratory discomfort or pain; and

    (k) Sputum production.

62. State when injured plaintiff/decedent was first diagnosed as suffering from an asbestos-related medical condition and include in your answer:

    (a) The date of such diagnosis;

    (b) The identity of the diagnosing physician and state whether said physician made positive finds of:

        (i) Fibrosis;

        (ii) Pleural plaques;

        (iii) Calcification;

(iv) Dysphea;

(v) Emphysema;

(vi) Tuberculosis; or

(vii) Disease grade (i.e., 1, 2, 3, 4) pneumonia.

(c) The identity of any health care institution or physician involved in any part of such diagnosis;

(d) The identity of every person, including injured plaintiff's/decedent's relatives, employer, or anyone acting on his behalf, to whom such diagnosis was made known, including the date, time and place, and the identity of anyone witnessing said revelation;

(e) Whether injured plaintiff/decedent continued to engage in any activity or occupation where he was exposed to asbestos materials after he was informed of such diagnosis;

(f) The course of treatment or therapy prescribed, including any medication, as a result of such diagnosis, and the identity of each prescribing physician;

(g) Whether injured plaintiff/decedent followed the treatment, medication or therapy regimen prescribed by each of the said physicians for the treatment of said diagnosed medical condition; and

(h) The identity of every physician subsequently affirming or making the same
diagnosis.

63. Did any of the physicians identified in response
to Interrogatory 62 inform injured plaintiff/dece-
dent at any time that his asbestos-related medical
condition may have been caused by factors other
than exposure to asbestos or asbestos-containing
products?

If your answer is yes, state:

(a) The other factors or reasons involved;

(b) The identity of the physicians so informing
injured plaintiff/decedent;

(c) The dates that said physician so informed
injured plaintiff/decedent; and

(d) State whether any such factors or reasons
were excluded as possible sources or causes
of the medical condition.

64. State the following with regard to injured plaintiff's/decedent's medical condition:

(a) The identity of each physician who treated,
examined or consulted with injured plain-
tiff/decedent, the dates of said treatment,
examination or consultation and any diagnosis made and the date of diagnosis;

(b) The identity of each health care institution
in which injured plaintiff/decedent was
confined, treated or examined, stating the
inclusive dates of any hospitalization
and/or the dates of any out-patient treat-

ment, the diagnosis made, the date of diagnosis, and the nature of the treatment; and

(c) If the inured plaintiff/decedent is presently under a physician's care for his medical condition(s), or was at the time of his death, state:

(i) The identity of each physician;

(ii) Any drugs or treatments prescribed by each physician; and

(iii) The dates of injured plaintiff's/decedent's visits or treatments.

65. If injured plaintiff/decedent ever had any medical symptoms, complaints, injuries, illnesses, accidents or operations or any medical complaints, injuries, illnesses or accidents requiring medical attention, other than those related to his asbestos-related medical condition(s), state with regard to each:

(a) Its nature and the dates thereof;

(b) The identity of each physician who treated, examined or consulted with injured plaintiff/decedent in each such instance, the dates of said treatment, examination or consultation and any diagnosis made;

(c) The identity of each health care institution in which injured plaintiff/decedent was confined, treated or examined, stating the inclusive dates of any hospitalization or the dates of any out-patient treatment, the diagnosis made, the date of diagnosis, and the nature of treatment; and

(d) The nature and extent of any permanent disabilities or residual effects.

66. If injured plaintiff/decedent ever underwent any periodic, pre-employment, employment-related, insurance-related, Armed Forces or National Guard medical or physical examinations, state as to each such examination:

    (a) The entity (including, but no limited to, any employer, union or insurance company) who offered, required, or sponsored such examination;

    (b) The dates and locations of each such examination;

    (c) The identity of the physician under whose supervision each examination was conducted; and

    (d) The nature and results of each such examination.

67. State any disease, injury or preexisting condition of health which you contend contributed to, or may have contributed to, injured plaintiff's/decedent's medical condition(s).

68. If you contend that injured plaintiff's/decedent's medical condition caused, or contributed to, the aggravation of any preexisting physical, nervous or mental condition, identify the preexisting condition and state the date injured plaintiff/decedent first became aware that his medical

condition had caused, or contributed to, an aggravation of any preexisting condition.

69. Describe any pain, incapacity, inability to lead a normal life, inability to work, or disability (including retirement) alleged to have resulted from injured plaintiff's/decedent's medical condition, including the date and basis therefor.

70. If you or your attorney have any medical reports from any persons or institution that ever treated or examined injured plaintiff/decedent at any time, provide copies of all of the reports.

   If you object to the production of copies of any reports, state for each report:

   (a) The identity of the report; and

   (b) The reason it was prepared.

71. Did injured plaintiff/decedent ever have any biopsies or tissue samples taken?

   If your answer is yes, state for each such procedure:

   (a) The identity of each physician performing such procedures;

   (b) The date and place of such procedures; and

   (c) The results, conclusions, and/or diagnoses arising from such procedures, and the dates on which injured plaintiff/decedent was advised of same.

72. Were any pathology slides made from any of injured plaintiff's/decedent's tissue samples at any time?

If your answer is yes, for each set of slides made, state:

(a) The identity of the Physician obtaining the tissue sample, the identity of the Health Care Institution where the tissue sample was obtained, and the date the tissue sample was obtained;

(b) The identity of the physician preparing the pathology slides, the identity of the health care institution where the slides were prepared, and the date the slides were prepared;

(c) The identity of all physicians who have analyzed the pathology slides, the identity of the health care institution where the analysis was done, and the date of the analysis;

(d) The results of said analysis;

(e) The conclusions and/or diagnoses arising from analysis of the pathology slides, and the dates on which injured plaintiff/decedent was advised of the results;

(f) The current location of said slides; and

(g) Provide appropriate authorization to view and/or obtain and made photographic reproductions of said slides.

73. Did injured plaintiff/decedent every have any chest, lung or other respiratory system x-rays taken?

If your answer is yes, state for each set of x-rays:

(a) If applicable, the identity of the physician ordering said x-rays;

(b) The identity of the place where said x-rays were taken and the date;

(c) The reason said x-rays were taken;

(d) The identity of all physicians who have read, analyzed or interpreted said x-rays;

(e) The results of said x-rays;

(f) The conclusions and/or diagnoses arising from such procedure, and the dates on which injured plaintiff/decedent was advised of the results;

(g) The location of all said x-ray films; and

(h) Provide appropriate authorization to view or obtain and make photographic reproduction of said x-rays.

74. Did injured plaintiff/decedent ever have any pulmonary function tests conducted?

If your answer is yes, state for each such test:

(a) If applicable, the identity of the physician ordering said test;

(b) The identity of the place where said test was conducted and the date;

(c) The reason said test was conducted;

(d) The identity of all physicians who analyzed or interpreted said tests;

(e) The results of said test;

(f) The conclusions and/or diagnoses arising from such tests, and the dates on which injured plaintiff/decedent was advised of the results; and

(g) The identity of the person who advised injured plaintiff/decedent of the results.

75. Did injured plaintiff/decedent ever consult with or was he ever seen professionally by a psychiatrist, psychologist or counselor?

If your answer is yes, state:

(a) The date of such consultation or visit; and

(b) If said consultation or visit occurred within the last ten years, or within ten years prior to decedent's death:

(i) The identity of the psychiatrist, psychologist or counselor; and

(ii) The reason for the consultation or visit.

76. If injured plaintiff/decedent was ever unable to work for more than one week due to a medical condition, describe for each such condition:

(a) The nature of the condition;

(b) The identity of injured plaintiff's/decedent's treating physician; and

(c) The dates of and length of time injured plaintiff/decedent was ill, disabled, or out or work.

77. Did injured plaintiff/decedent every make any claim for, or receive any, health or accident insurance benefits, Social Security benefits, state or federal benefits for disability, workers' compensation benefits, veterans' benefits, tort claims or suits, Federal Employers Liability Act claims or suits, Longshoremen and Harbor Workers Act claims or suits, unemployment compensation insurance benefits, or early payment from any public or private pensions due to disability or his medical condition?

If your answer is yes, state:

(a) The date and place where such claim was made;

(b) The identity of the entity with which the claim was made;

(c) Any identifying number, such as a docket number, for each claim;

(d) The defendant, agency, insurer, employer or other entity to or against whom the claim was made;

(e) The nature of the claim; and

(f) The result of such claim, including any amount received by way of settlement, judgment or award upon the claim.

78. Was a death certificate prepared after the death of the decedent?

If your answer is yes, attach a copy to your responses to these Interrogatories.

To the extent the death certificate does not so indicate, state:

(a) Whether it was filed?

(b) The identity of the office in which it was filed;

(c) The identity of the person listed on the certificate as the informant;

(d) The relationship of the person listed as the informant to or connection with the decedent;

(e) The identity and professional specialty or each physician furnishing the information appearing on the death certificate;

(f) The immediate cause of death; and

(g) The exact time, date and place of death.

79. Was an autopsy performed on the body of the decedent?

If your answer is yes, state for each autopsy:

(a) The identity and official capacity of each person authorizing or ordering the autopsy;

(b) The relationship to or connection with the decedent of each person authorizing or ordering the autopsy;

(c) Why the autopsy was ordered;

(d) The identity and professional specialty of each person performing the autopsy;

(e) The date, time and place the autopsy was performed;

(f) The cause of death shown by the autopsy;

(g) The identity and occupation of each person having custody of the report of the results of the autopsy; and

(h) Attach a copy of each autopsy report to your responses to these interrogatories or execute and provide appropriate authorizations to examine and obtain photocopies of said autopsy reports.

I. DAMAGES

80. State, in the form of an itemized list, all special damages alleged in this lawsuit, including, but not limited to, physician's services, health care institution expenses, ambulance expenses, x-rays, diagnostic tests, prescription drugs, physiotherapy, psychiatric services, and lost wages, and identify the person or organization to whom each item expense was paid or due, and by whom each item of expense was paid.

If there is any lien on the damages the plaintiff is claiming, identify the lienholder and state the total amount of lien.

81. If you are making a claim for loss of earnings or impairment of earning power because of injured plaintiff's/decedent's medical condition, state:

(a) The identity of injured plaintiff's/decedent's employer, job classification and monthly or weekly rate of pay at the time of the onset of his medical condition;

(b) Whether injured plaintiff/decedent had more than one employer during the three-year period prior to the date of the onset of his medical condition, and if your answer is yes, identify each such employer, other than the one stated above, and injured plaintiff's/decedent's job classification, monthly or weekly rate of pay, and inclusive dates of such employment during the three year period;

(c) Injured plaintiff's/decedent's total earnings for the period of three years prior to the onset of his medical condition;

(d) The inclusive dates during which you allege that injured plaintiff/decedent was unable to work as a result of his medical condition and the total amount of pay you claim he lost because of his absence;

(e) The date on which injured plaintiff/decedent started work again; and

(f) The name and address of each employer for whom injured plaintiff's decedent worked, with inclusive dates of employment and indicating whether retired, each job classification injured plaintiff/decedent held and each monthly or weekly rate of pay which he received, from the date he first started working again after the onset of his medical condition through the present time, or to the time of death.

82. Do you claim damages for loss of consortium, society, affection, services, or sexual enjoyment?

If your answer is yes, set forth all facts on which this claim is based, including a complete description of the loss suffered. As to the alleged lost services, additionally provide:

(a) The duration of the loss of any service; and

(b) The cost, if any, incurred to obtain substitute services.

83. State fully and in detail the annual earnings for the past ten years, or the ten years prior to death, for injured plaintiff/decedent and injured plaintiff's/decedent's spouse.

84. Do you have access to injured plaintiff's/decedent's W-2 forms and income tax returns for the last ten years or the ten years prior to death?

If your answer is yes, attach copies to your responses to these Interrogatories.

If not available, execute and provide a release in form acceptable to the Internal Revenue Service to obtain copies of said tax records.

85. Itemize the expenses incurred in connection with the funeral, burial, cremation or other means of attending to the decedent's remains.

86. Did the decedent die testate?

If your answer is yes, state:

(a) The date the will and each codicil was executed;

(b) Details of any attempts to revoke or invalidate the will;

(c) Whether the will has been filed for probate and, if so, the date and place;

(d) The identity of each executor named in the will;

(e) Whether the estate is still in probate;

(f) The identity of and relationship to the decedent of each beneficiary named in the will and the bequest or devise made to each;

(g) The identity of each attorney of record to the probate of the will; and

(h) Attach a copy of each will and codicil to your responses to these interrogatories.

87. Has there been a contest of the will of the decedent?

If your answer is yes, state:

(a) The identity of and relationship to the decedent of each person contesting the will;

(b) The date the contest was filed;

(c) The name of the court and the title and file number of the contest;

(d) The grounds for contesting the will; and

(e) How and when the contest was determined by the court.

88. Did the decedent die intestate?

If your answer is yes, state:

(a) Whether there is necessity for administration of the decedent's estate;

(b) Whether an application for administration has been filed and, if so, the date, name of the court, and the title of proceeding and file number;

(c) The identity of each duly qualified and appointed administrator of the estate;

(d) Whether the estate is still being administered;

(e) Whether any Letters of Administration (general or special) were ever issued in connection with the decedent's estate, and if so, attach copies of such Letters to your responses to these Interrogatories;

(f) The date on which Letters of Administration were issued to said administrator;

(g) The court, name of the Judge and the clerk issuing said Letters of Administration;

(h) Whether there were any limitations or restrictions placed on said Letters of Administration, and if so, the nature of those limitations or restrictions;

(i) Whether any court has issued Letters of Administration and subsequently suspended, modified or revoked them and, if so, set forth the circumstances;

(j) Whether Letters of Administration or Letters Testamentary have every been issued to any persons other than those identified in (c), above and if so, set forth the circumstances;

(k) Whether there were any objections filed to any application for Letters of Administration, and if so, set forth the circumstances; and

(l) Whether any bond was posted in order to qualify as administrator, and if so, attach a copy to your responses to these interrogatories.

89. Has there been a proceeding to determine the heirs of the decedent's estate?

If your answer is yes, state:

(a) The name of the court and the titled of the proceeding and file number;

(b) The date of commencement of the proceeding;

(c) The date the order adjudicating heirship was rendered;

(d) Whether there has been an appeal from such order;

(e) Whether such order has ever been altered, amended or reversed; and

(f) The identity of and relationship to decedent and extent of right to inherit from the decedent of each heir as determined by this proceeding.

90. If you are suing on behalf of the decedent or the decedent's estate, or if you are the personal representative of the decedent, attach copies of the papers which authorize you to maintain this action.

91. If it is claimed that any damages are owing to any person or entity on account of loss of an inheritance as a result of decedent's alleged exposure to asbestos or asbestos-containing products:

(a) State the decedent's net worth at the time of death;

(b) List all real and personal property owned by the decedent at the time of the decedent's death and where the same was located (clothing and personal effects need not be included); and

(c) Indicate all bank savings accounts maintained in the name of the decedent, indicating with respect to each:

(i) The identity of the bank;

(ii) The account number; and

(iii) The amount in the account at the time of the decedent's death.

92. Has an estate tax return been filed by the decedent's estate?

If your answer is yes:

(a) State the identity of the person or firm that prepared the return; and

(b) Identify the present custodian of the return.

93. Do you have or have access to the decedent's estate tax return?

If your answer is yes, attach a copy to your response to these Interrogatories.

If not available, execute and provide a release in a form acceptable to the Internal Revenue Service to obtain a copy of said tax record.

94. During the last five years of the decedent's life, did anyone other than the decedent contribute to the decedent's support?

If your answer is yes, state as to each:

(a) His identity and relationship to or connection with the decedent;

(b) The amount of each contribution, specifying whether in money, services, gifts or other forms; and

(c) The annual amount of such contributions.

95. During the last five years of the decedent's life, did anyone other than the decedent contribute to the support of any of the decedent's immediate family?

If your answer is yes, state as to each:

(a) The identity and relationship of each relative receiving such support;

(b) The identity of each person, other than the decedent, who contributed to each person, other than the decedent, who contributed to each relative's support;

(c) The amount of each contribution, specifying whether in money, services, gifts, or other forms; and

(d) The annual amount of such contributions.

96. During the last ten years of his life, did the decedent contribute money or other tangible benefits to any of his children, spouses, former spouse(s), or parents?

If your answer is yes, state for each such person:

(a) His identity and relationship to decedent;

(b) The date and place of birth;

(c) The date of each contribution;

(d) The reason for each contribution;

(e) The amount or value of each contribution;

(f) A description of anything of value decedent received in exchange for such contribution; and

(g) The years for which decedent claimed this person as a dependent for income tax purposes.

97. During the last ten years of his life, did decedent ever contribute to the support of persons other than his children, spouse, former spouse(s) or parents?

If your answer is yes, state for each such person:

(a) His identity and relationship to decedent;

(b) The date and place of birth;

(c) The date of each contribution;

(d) The reason for each contribution;

(e) The amount or value of each contribution;

(f) A description of anything of value decedent received in exchange for such contribution; and

(g) The years for which decedent claimed this person as a dependent for income tax purposes.

98. Did the decedent perform services for any of his children, spouses, former spouse(s) or parents?

If your answer is yes, state for each person:

(a) The identity and relationship to the decedent of the person for whom the service was performed;

(b) A description of each service performed for such person;

(c) The total time spent by the decedent performing the service per year and the frequency with which he performed such service;

(d) The date the decedent last performed each such service;

(e) The compensation, if any, the decedent received for performing each service;

(f) The identity and relationship to the decedent of each person or agency compensating the decedent for each service;

(g) The total cost to such person of getting others to perform each service performed by the decedent; and

(h) The identity and occupation of each person performing each such service since the decedent's death.

J. MISCELLANEOUS

99. Identify and give the substance of all written statements, recordings, or videotapes which relate to the facts of this lawsuit and the alleged damages given by you, injured plaintiff/decedent or any witness.

100. Have you or did injured plaintiff/decedent have any written or oral communication with any defendant?

If your answer is yes, state with respect to each defendant:

(a) Whether you were and/or the injured plaintiff/decedent was a party to such communication;

(b) The sum and substance of each such communication;

(c) The date and exact location of each;

(d) Whether such communication was written or oral, and, if written, annex a copy of same to your response to these interrogatories;

(e) The identity of or if not known, a description of such defendant or its employees, agents and/or servants with whom the communication was had; and

(f) The identity of or, if not known, a description of each witness to each such oral communication.

101. Have you or did injured plaintiff/decedent give or send to any defendant or have you or did the injured plaintiff/decedent receive from any defendant any written communication?

If your answer is yes:

(a) State as to each:

(i) The identity of the person who gave or sent such communication;

(ii) The identity of the person who received such communication;

(iii) The date of such communication;

(iv) The identity of the present custodian of such communication; and

(b) Annex a copy of each such communication to your response to these Interrogatories.

102. Have you, did injured plaintiff/decedent, or has anyone acting on behalf of you or injured plaintiff/decedent obtained any statements, either written or recorded, from any defendant or from any person in the employ of any defendant with respect to the occurrences alleged in the complaint?

If your answer is yes:

(a) State as to each:

    (i) Who obtained such statement;

    (ii) The identity of the person from whom such statement was obtained;

    (iii) The date such statement was obtained;

    (iv) The sum and substance of such statement;

    (v) The identity of the present custodian of such statement; or

(b) Annex a copy of each such communication to your response to these Interrogatories.

103. State separately as to each defendant the identity of and, if known, the Social Security numbers of all potential witnesses who may give testimony concerning injured plaintiff's/decedent's alleged exposure to and/or the manufacture and sale of asbestos materials and asbestos-containing products.

104. Identify all persons, except experts, on whose testimony plaintiff intends to rely at trial.

105. With regard to each person whom the plaintiff expects to call as an expert witness at trial, provide a copy of the witness' curriculum vitae or a summary of the witness' qualifications and state for each such expert witness:

(a) His identity;

(b) The subject matter on which such expert is to testify;

(c) The substance of all facts and opinions regarding which such expert is to testify;

(d) A summary of the grounds for each opinion of such expert;

(e) Whether the facts and opinions listed in (c) above are contained in a written report, memorandum or transcript;

(f) Whether such expert intends to base his testimony on any book, treatise, article, study, or any other document, and if so, identify all such documents; and

(g) Whether the witness has testified at trial or by deposition in other asbestos-related personal injury or wrongful death cases, and if so, state for each such case:

(i) The name and docket number;

(ii) The court in which each such case is or was pending; and

(iii) The identity of the party for whom the witness testified.

106. Identify all persons, other than your attorneys, who provided you with any information used in answering these interrogatories, and state the particular information each person supplied.

REQUEST FOR PRODUCTION OF DOCUMENTS

Pursuant to Rule 3120 of the Civil Practice Law and Rules of New York State, the defendants request that plaintiffs produce for inspection and copying at such time as the responses to the interrogatories herein are filed, the following documents for discovery, inspection and copying:

1. All documents identified in your responses to these Interrogatories.

2. All documents relating to injured plaintiff's/decedent's job qualifications and professional licenses held.

3. All documents relating to injured plaintiff's/decedent's employment.

4. All documents relating to injured plaintiff's/decedent's membership in any labor trade association or professional organization.

5. All documents relating to injured plaintiff's/decedent's military or foreign service, including and not limited to personnel records, discharge papers, military occupational specialty qualifications, promotions, reductions or disciplinary actions.

6. All documents relating to any claim or demand ever made by injured plaintiff/decedent for damages, compensation or other benefits allegedly

resulting from any illness or injury, including but not limited to Workers' Compensation Board records, federal or state employment compensation claim records, Social Security disability records, pension claim records or any other health or accident insurance claim records.

7. All documents, relating to the subject matter of this lawsuit, of which you have ever become aware, relating in any way to meetings, correspondence, statements or other communications of or from any manufacturer or supplier of asbestos, asbestos-containing products and/or asbestos-containing material or from their agents or representatives.

8. All documents, relating to the subject matter of this lawsuit, of which you have ever become aware, relating in any way to meetings, correspondence or other communications of or from any trade association, labor union, employer or governmental agency, of or from any of their agents or representatives, relating to the subjects of occupational health and exposure to asbestos, asbestos-containing products and/or asbestos-containing materials.

9. All documents prepared by or on behalf of the plaintiff or decedent, prior to this litigation, in any way relating to the documents request in item Nos. 5 and 6, above, of this request for production.

10. All documents relating in any way to injured plaintiff's/decedent's exposure or possible exposure to asbestos, asbestos-containing products and/or asbestos-containing materials.

11. All documents relating in any way to injured plaintiff's/decedent's exposures to substances identified in Interrogatory 18.

12. All documents relating in any way to any asbestos, asbestos-containing products and/or asbestos-containing materials manufactured, distributed and/or supplied by any person or entity or by any of the names defendants herein to which you claim injured plaintiff/decedent applied or was exposed.

13. All documents, of which you have ever become aware, relating in any way to warnings, potential health hazards, instructions or precautions regarding the use or handling of, or exposure to, asbestos, asbestos-containing products, and/or asbestos-containing materials.

14. All applications prepared or submitted by or on behalf of injured plaintiff/decedent for life insurance, medical insurance, health and accident insurance, and/or disability insurance.

15. All statements, recorded interviews, films, videotapes, reports, questionnaires, forms or other documents made, submitted, compiled, prepared or filled out by, on behalf of, or under the direction of, plaintiff or decedent relating in any way to exposure or alleged exposure to asbestos, asbestos-containing products and/or asbestos-containing materials or any other issues relating to this lawsuit, except that information prepared by, for, or at the request of plaintiff's counsel must be identified (including the date made), but need not be produced without an Order by the Court, provided that written or recorded commu-

nication between plaintiff and counsel, made after an attorney-client relationship has been established need not be produced or identified.

16. All documents relating to injured plaintiff's/decedent's first knowledge, notice or awareness about the alleged adverse effects of exposure to asbestos, asbestos-containing products and/or asbestos-containing materials.

17. All records relating to comments, complaints, suggestions, or proposals made to injured plaintiff's/decedent's union, by injured plaintiff/decedent or by other employees or union members regarding asbestos exposure.

18. All written, recorded, filmed, transcribed or videotaped statements of all parties and nonparty declarant pertaining to the subject to this lawsuit, except as to non-party declarant that information prepared by, for, or at the request of plaintiff's counsel must be identified (including the date made), but need not be produced without an Order by the Court, provided that written or recorded communication between plaintiff and counsel, made after an attorney-client relationship has been established need not be produced or identified.

19. All photographs of injured plaintiff/decedent at work or in work clothes and all photographs of all products or conditions complained of in injured plaintiff's/decedent's place of employment.

20. Copies of all itemized bills covering all the special damages and losses and expenses claimed in this matter.

21. Copies of all reports, correspondence and records from any doctor who has examined injured plaintiff/decedent, any hospital where injured plaintiff/decedent was treated either as an in-patient or as an out-patient, except for any reports, records, correspondence, or communications issued by any consulting physicians who have been retained or specially employed in anticipation of litigation or preparation for trial and who are not expected to be called as witnesses at trial.

22. All tissue specimens, tissue slides, and x-rays films pertaining to injured plaintiff/decedent.

23. Copies of injured plaintiff's/decedent's income tax records for the last ten years, or for ten years prior to his death, as well as any other documents including economic loss reports, upon which plaintiff relies in support of his claims. If loss of earnings or earning capacity is alleged or claimed to have occurred before the current year, include copies of the income tax returns of injured plaintiff/decedent from ten years prior to the claimed loss and up to the current tax year, or the year of death.

24. Any asbestos materials and/or asbestos-containing products of the type to which injured plaintiff/decedent allegedly was exposed and which plaintiff has in his possession, custody or control.

25. All photographs, charts, drawings, diagrams or other graphic representations depicting work conditions and sites where injured plaintiff/decedent was allegedly exposed to asbestos or asbestos-containing products.

26. All boxes, containers or wrappers that allegedly contained the asbestos materials and/or asbestos-containing products which are the subject of plaintiff's Complaint and which are in the plaintiff's or plaintiff's attorney's possession, custody or control.

27. All labels, tags, or warnings on the boxes, containers or wrappers which allegedly contained asbestos materials and/or asbestos-containing products, which are the subject of plaintiff's complaint and which are in plaintiff's or plaintiff's attorney's possession, custody or control.

28. All invoices, bills, statements and any other writing or records which plaintiff contends evidence the sale of any products containing asbestos to the place of injured plaintiff's/decedent's employment at which injured plaintiff/decedent was allegedly exposed to asbestos.

29. Any written advice, publication, warning, order, directive, requirement, or recommendation, which advised or warned of the possible harmful effects of exposure to or inhalation of asbestos materials and/or asbestos-containing products in the possession, custody or control of the plaintiff which came into the possession, custody or control of the injured plaintiff/decedent during alleged period of exposure.

30. Any accident or incident reports which relate to the facts, circumstances or incidents which form the basis of plaintiff's Complaint.

31. Any written statements given by the plaintiff or the decedent which relate to facts, circumstances, incidents, injuries or damages which form the basis of plaintiff's Complaint, including but not limited to statements made to any police or law enforcement officers, insurance company representatives, state or federal agents, or representatives or employees of other companies.

DATED:

SAMPLE AFFIDAVIT

AFFIDAVIT

STATE OF [*state*]   )

                                   SS:

COUNTY OF [*sounty*]   )

NOW COMES [*name of administrator*], who being duly sworn, makes oath as follows:

1. That [*client came*] had worked as [*list appropriate job titles*].

2. That as part of such work he had been exposed to asbestos-containing insulation materials and have breathed air containing particles of dust arising from such materials.

3. That to my knowledge he had used and been exposed to asbestos-containing insulation products manufactured, sold, or distributed by [*company name*] or its divisions or subsidiaries only in the following particulars:

<u>JOB SITE   EMPLOYER   DATE   ACTIVITY</u>

[*fill in specific information as to employers, job site, dates of employment and job titles*]

4. That he was not an employee of [*company name*] on any of the jobs listed above in paragraph No. 3.

5. That he suffered from asbestosis and/or other illnesses associated with asbestos as evidenced by the findings of a medical doctor contained in a report [*attached hereto as Exhibit 1 or previously submitted*].

6. That this affidavit is made a representation to [*company name*] to induce it to make a money payment to settle

his claim for damages against it and its predecessors, successors, divisions, subsidiaries, officers, agent, and employees, but not against any other persons.

7. [*client name*] was [*marital status*] at the time of his death, and his wife's name is [*spouse's name*].

8. He was born on [*date of birth*]; his social security number is [*social security number*].

9. I authorize said settlement to be effected by payment to [*client's name, with spouse's if married*] estate and Shapiro & Shapiro, his attorney, and represent that his fiduciary will execute all documents necessary to discharge [*company name*], its predecessors, successors, divisions, subsidiaries, officers, agents and employees, against further claims by his estate, or future claims by his statutory beneficiaries, heirs, and the representative of the estate, and his statutory beneficiaries, heirs, and the representative of his estate will indemnify injury or damage to his estate, heirs, or statutory beneficiaries by virtue of any asbestos related disease or death.

10. The date on which he was first diagnosed or had a reason to believe he was suffering from an asbestos related disease was [*date of diagnosis*].

_____ ____
[*client name*]

Sworn To and Subscribed Before Me the _____ Day of
_____, 19___ .
My commission expires ____/____/____ .

_____
NOTARY PUBLIC

GENERAL RELEASE

KNOW YE, That I, [*client name*], residing at [*client address*], for and in consideration of the sum of [*amount of settlement written out*] dollars ($ [*amount in numbers*]), lawful money of the United States of America to me in hand paid by

[*defendant(s) name(s)*]

the receipt whereof is hereby acknowledged, have remised, released, and forever discharged and by these presents do I for myself and my heirs, executors and administrators, remise, release and forever discharge the said

[*defendant(s) name(s)*]

successors and assigns, heirs, executors and administrators, of and from all, and all manner of action and actions, cause and causes of action, suits, debts, dues, sums of money, accounts reckoning, bonds, bills specialties, covenants, contracts, controversies, agreements, promises, variances, trespasses, damages, judgments, extents executions, claims and demands whatsoever, in law or in equity, which against the said

[*defendant(s) name(s)*]

I ever had, now have or which heirs, executors or administrators hereafter can, shall or may have for, upon or by reason of any matter, cause or thing whatsoever.

The above Release pertains to an asbestos exposure which occurred on or about [*date*].

IN WITNESS WHEREOF have hereunto set my hand and seal the _____ day of _____, in the year Nineteen Hundred and _____.

[L.S.]   _____
          [*client name*]

STATE OF [*state*]   )
                                   SS:
COUNTY OF [*county*]   )

On the _____ day of _____, 19___ personally appeared [*client name*] to me known and known to me to be the same person described in and who executed the within instrument and [*he* or *she*] acknowledged to me that [*he* or *she*] executed the same.

          _____ _____
          NOTARY PUBLIC

SILICONE IMPLANTS

Silicone implants have been available for over 25 years. Such implants are commonly comprised of a shell made of elasticized silicone, and a filling of silicone gel. The most widely marketed type of silicone implants are breast implants, which have been used for both cosmetic enhancement of the breasts, and for reconstruction after breast surgery.

Silicone implants have been associated with physical problems that are both localized (related to the breast only) and systemic (related to the whole body).

An implant is a foreign substance to the human body. When a foreign substance is introduced into the body, the body's normal response is to isolate that substance. This reaction results in the formation of hard capsules around the silicone implants. This hardening frequently creates an unnatural firmness to the breasts, and extreme discomfort to the implant recipient.

Many implants are susceptible to ruptures while inside of the recipient's body. When an implant ruptures, it allows silicone gel contained within the implant to escape. While such escaped silicone gel may be confined within the hard capsule that forms around the implant, it may also migrate to other parts of the body. Further, ruptures frequently cause cosmetic deformities, such as indentation or movement of the implant.

Another means by which silicone may leave the implant is through gel bleed. Gel bleed has been shown to occur with virtually all silicone implants. Gel bleed occurs when tiny beads of the silicone gel encased in the implant's silicone envelope seep out, even though there may be no distinct rupture. It is believed that after a period of time, these seepages of silicone enter the body.

Silicone is believed to create adverse effects to the immune system, thereby causing the implant recipient to experience symptoms including:

- extreme fatigue;

- joint and muscle pain;

- hair loss;

- dryness of eyes and mouth;

- numbness in extremities;

- memory loss

Silicone implants have also been associated with serious autoimmune diseases, including lupus and scleroderma. Further, silicone implants may be a factor in neurological disorders and some cancers.

Long before silicone implants were placed on the market, implant manufacturers' own research disclosed that silicone could cause serious health problems. Despite such findings, the manufacturers chose to aggressively market silicone implants to plastic surgeons and to the general public.

Silicone has also been used in a number of other medical devices. Such devices include artificial joints, dental implants, and cosmetic implants to enhance or restore the shape of other body parts. Further, silicone has been used in direct injections to enhance body parts, particularly facial features such as the cheeks and lips.

If you have been exposed to silicone or silicone implants, and believe that you have sustained injuries as a result, you may wish to consult an attorney. You may have a right to recover against the manufacturers of your implants, and in some cases, a claim for medical malpractice against the physician who performed the implant surgery.

Before meeting with the attorney, you should gather information including the name of the physician and facility where you obtained the implants, date of implant surgery, and any records that you possess pertaining to this surgery. Of particular importance is any information that identifies the manufacturer of your implants. You can also assist your attorney by preparing a list of the names and addresses of all physicians and other medical care providers with whom you have treated or consulted since obtaining your implants.

If you believe that you have been injured as a result of silicone implants, you should not delay in consulting a lawyer to learn of your legal rights to recover. Failure to bring action within the statute of limitations, a time deadline set by law, could result in the loss of any rights that you have to recover. This means that no matter how serious your injuries, you could receive no money if your case is not filed before the statute of limitations expires.

ELECTROMAGNETIC FIELDS

Research has suggested a connection between electromagnetic fields and certain cancers, particularly leukemia in children. Studies have shown that children living in close proximity to power lines can be up to ten percent (10%) more likely to develop leukemia than children who do not have such exposure.

Electromagnetic fields are created by virtually all electronic devices, but toxic exposure is primarily associated with extended exposure to power lines. Devices that emit large amounts of electromagnetic radiation have also been suspected in creating toxic exposures.

If you believe that you or your family are currently being exposed to electromagnetic fields, testing is available. Utility companies may offer to perform such testing, but such companies may wish to downplay the significance of electromagnetic field exposure. It may therefore be advisable to obtain such testing through an independent agency.

If you believe that you or a family member has been damaged by exposure to electromagnetic fields, you may wish to seek legal advice. The attorney with whom you consult may be able to assist you in obtaining the information necessary to document your claim. You may be asked many questions with regard to your family's health history, as well as questions about the health of other individuals who reside in your neighborhood. Information showing an increased incidence of cancers or other serious health problems among residents of an area located in close proximity to power lines or other sources of electromagnetic radiation, will assist the attorney in proceeding with the potential claim.

As with any legal claim, a case against a power company or other source of electromagnetic fields must be commenced within a specific amount of time. By consulting with an attorney immediately, you will learn your rights with regard to the applicable statute of limitations for your case.

LEAD

Until the early 1970's, lead was commonly used as a base for paints used in the interior and exterior of many homes. Lead has been shown to have toxic effects when taken into the body. Those most commonly affected by lead poisoning are young children, who may ingest tiny chips of lead or inhale airborne lead particles.

If you live in an older home or apartment, lead paint may be present. Common places where lead paint may be found include window frames and sills, door frames, porch floors, and walls. Merely living in an environment where lead paint has been used will not harm you. Lead is only harmful if it is ingested or inhaled. Further, amounts of lead that may not be harmful to adults may be highly toxic to children, because of their smaller body size and developing nervous systems. Likewise, pregnant women should avoid exposure to lead, as such exposure may harm the developing fetus.

Common symptoms associated with children's exposure to lead based paint include listlessness, inability to concentrate, uncontrollable behavior, learning disabilities, hyperactivity, nausea, and loss of appetite. In extreme cases, children may suffer damage to their internal organs, including the brain, as a result of exposure to lead.

Many children are routinely checked for lead in their blood when they are seen by their pediatrician. If routine testing discloses the presence of lead, treatments including hospitalization for chelation therapy, or medications administered at home may be prescribed.

In some areas, the discovery of lead in a child's system is automatically reported to the local health department. The health department will notify the owner of the property that a child living on the premises has been found to have lead in their system. An inspection of the premises will be conducted, and areas where lead hazards exist will be identified. The property owner will then be required to remove, or abate, the lead hazard before the child can resume residence.

If lead is discovered in your home, you should not seek to remove it before seeking professional advice on a safe and effective way to do so. Your local health department may be able to provide you with guidelines for removing lead based paints; trained professionals also provide lead abatement services. Prior to undertaking any lead abatement project, you should be sure that all children and pets are removed from the area, and once the removal has been completed, the area should be thoroughly cleaned to remove any excess lead dust.

You should also be aware that lead may be present in plumbing lines that supply water to some residences. If you believe that lead is present in your water supply, you should contact your local water authority, or an independent plumber for advice.

Lead may also be present in the soil surrounding your home. For this reason, it is important to supervise young children when they play outdoors, to make sure that they are not ingesting soil which may contain lead. Finally, some types of pottery-type dishes may contain lead, particularly if such pottery was manufactured outside of the United States. Before purchasing or using such dishes, you should check to make sure that there is no lead content, and if in doubt, do not use such dishes for serving food.

If you believe that your child has been exposed to lead, you should bring this fact immediately to the attention of your child's pediatrician. Should testing disclose that there is lead in the child's bloodstream, the child should immediately be removed from the environment where exposure occurred. All instructions from the pediatrician regarding the child's medical care should be precisely followed, and the child's behavioral and physical changes should be closely monitored.

To protect your child from lead before such exposure occurs, you should ask your landlord to verify in writing that there is no lead present on the property. Likewise, if you are purchasing a home, you should have an inspection performed and obtain verification that no lead hazard exists. If you observe peeling paint, paint chips, or crumbling plaster on any area of the property, you should immediately provide written notification to the landlord of the existence of this condition, and of your expectation that it be fixed as soon as possible. If the condition is not remedied, you should contact your local Department of Health and/or Building Code Enforcement Department. If you fail to provide such notification, and your child is later diagnosed with lead exposure, your failure to take action may weaken your case.

TOBACCO

In 1964, the U.S. government released findings linking tobacco with lung cancer and risks associated with other health risks. Since that time, the risks associated with smoking have gained increasing recognition. Before 1964, many tobacco companies claimed that their products could actually enhance the health of users. Once these claims regarding the health benefits of tobacco were shown to be false, some smokers and former smokers who had developed serious health problems brought legal action against tobacco companies. These cases alleged that the injured people tried cigarettes based on advertisements that touted cigarettes' health benefits, then became addicted and could not break the addiction even after the health risks were disclosed.

Such cases did not meet with success. The tobacco companies, some of the largest and most powerful corporations in the country, worked hard to defeat these claims.

Later, however, the Food and Drug Administration investigated the tobacco companies. This investigation disclosed that tobacco companies intentionally put large amounts of nicotine in cigarettes, in order to make cigarettes highly addictive. In addition, this investigation showed that the tobacco companies withheld research that showed the addictive nature of nicotine from the general public. Further, cigarette manufacturers often target their advertising at very young people in an effort to create addictions that begin early, and last long into adulthood. This information may provide the foundation upon which claims for injuries due to smoking may be brought against tobacco companies.

If you are a smoker or former smoker, you may have sustained damage due to tobacco company misrepresentations and fraud regarding the addictive nature of nicotine. If you have sustained serious injuries—such as lung cancer, emphysema, or death of a family member who smoked—you may wish to consult with an attorney to investigate the possibility of a legal claim.

Information that may assist your lawyer in evaluation your potential claim might include your reasons for starting to smoke, your age at the time you became a smoker, the amount of cigarettes that you smoke per day (and whether this amount has increased over time), the brand of cigarette that you smoke, whether you have tried to stop smoking (and with what results), and your physical problems that you associate with smoking.

Some people may believe that they understood the risks of smoking, and must therefore accept the health consequences. But even if some of the you understood risks associated with smoking, the manufacturers' wilful failure to disclose information about the addictive nature of their products may have prevented you from understanding all of the risks. Furthermore, the highly addictive nature of nicotine may have kept you smoking even after you recognized that cigarettes were harming you.

You should not automatically conclude that you assumed all of the risks of your cigarette or tobacco use. Reviewing your potential claim with an attorney may help you to understand what risks you assumed, and what risks the tobacco manufacturers intentionally kept from you.

James J. Shapiro with Leeza Gibbons

45 here join $5 billion suit

Claim injuries from implants

By Corydon Ireland

A Rochester law firm this week filed 100 lawsuits seeking up to $5 billion on behalf of New York women claiming injuries from silicone breast implants.

Forty-five of the women are from Monroe County. The others are from New York, Richmond, Erie, Niagara, Oneida and Onondaga counties, said an attorney from the firm, Shapiro and Shapiro.

The lawsuits were filed in state supreme courts in each county yesterday and Monday. They claim fraud, negligence and the violation of product safety laws, naming Dow Corning Corp., McGhan Medical Minnesota Minning and Manufacturing, Corp., Bristol-Meyers Squibb, Baxter Healthcare Corp. and other companies responsible for making the devices. Attorneys for Dow, McGhan and 3M Corp. did not return phone calls last night.

The 100 women claim injuries from the implants, including breast cancer, lymphoma, debilitating fatigue, joint and muscle pain, hardening of breast tissue, hair loss, numbness and discoloration of the extremities and lupus erythematosus, a disease in which the immune system attacks itself.

Other physical injuries claimed are "more diffuse, but still problematic," said Lori J. Henkel, lead attorney in the lawsuits.

In addition, the suits claim emotional suffering, loss of quality of life and "derivative actions" on behalf of affected spouses.

"I feel strongly that there was wrong done to my clients," said Henkel. "There was a great deal of information not disclosed to women for what appears to be a profit motive on the part of these companies."

A separate class action suite is under way against Dow and others in an Alabama federal court. Approximately 12,000 women will share a $1.5 billion compensation fund.

Henkel represents an additional 200 clients statewide who are taking part in the class action suit— "an excellent one for most of my clients," said Henkel. "The others want their day in court. They want to see these corporations brought to justice."

The 100 clients who filed separate civil actions this week felt the class action suit would not compensate them well enough for their injuries, Henkel said.

Compensation in the class action suit depends on a complicated formula that factors in age, illness and severity of illness. Likely class action awards range from $200,000 to $2 million for each victim.

This week's New York suites, filled at a cost of $170 apiece, could net each woman $50 million.

Lawsuits settled in April against McGhan Medical and others in Harrision County, Texas, won three women $5 million each in punitive damages. The three also won $12.9 million in other "actual" damages.

Miami Herald, Broward County edition, January 3, 1996

South Florida buyer eyes Panthers

By Donna Leinwand and Karen Rafinski

A local attorney and some undisclosed partners want to buy the Panthers hockey team and keep it in South Florida.

James Shapiro, a prominent personal injury attorney with offices in Hollywood [FL] and New York [State], and a nephew to Tampa Bay Buccaneers owner Malcolm Glazer, made an offer to Panthers owner H. Wayne Huizenga on Tuesday—$75 million cash.

Talk of moving the team out of Florida "just outrages me," Shapiro, 38, said from his Boca Raton home. "I want to keep the team in South Florida."

Huizenga spokesman Stan Smith confirmed that the offer had been made but wouldn't discuss it. He said the Panthers had turned the proposal over to the National Hockey League as it has done with three offers from out-of-state groups.

Shapiro's proposal represents the first time a local investor has made a formal offer to keep the team in the area since Huizenga imposed a Feb. 1 deadline. Huizenga said that if Broward County did not agree to build an arena by that date—and if a local owner did not come forward—he would sell the team to an out-of-town buyer.

Palm Beach businessman Bruce Frey has said he is putting together a group of investors, but apparently has not made a formal offer.

Shapiro said he had fewer than 10 investors but would not name them. Nor would he disclose whether his un-

cle is involved in the deal. Glazer told The Herald last week he had no interest in the Panthers.

"We have the money, but I'm not going to do it unless it makes financial sense," said Shapiro, who wants to review the team's books.

And it will probably take an agreement for a new arena to make the deal economically feasible, he said. "I believe it should be in Broward County. That's what my heart says. That doesn't mean that's the way it's going to be."

Adam Smith, an attorney for the investors, spoke with Huizenga Holdings President Richard Rochon about the offer Tuesday morning, said investor Fred Chikovsky.

From Rochon, Smith learned that Huizenga is losing about $1.5 million a month on the Panthers. By years end, that would raise the asking price from $75 million to more than $90 million.

"He said Mr. Huizenga is looking to get out what they put in," Smith said. "But we really did not discuss numbers."

Shapiro has no other sports investments or experience—and said he didn't know if any of his investors did either. But he said he has wanted to buy a team since his uncle purchased the Tampa Bay Buccaneers.

He stepped forward when it seemed no one else was willing to buy the team and keep it in South Florida. "I feel like I'll be helping the community," said Shapiro. "It'll be a lot of fun."

Shapiro started his four-lawyer firm, Shapiro & Shapiro, which has an office in Hollywood, with his father 12 years ago. They have handled numerous asbestos suits and filed $5 billion in claims against breast implant maker Dow Corning, Shapiro said.

Shapiro plans to begin courting politicians in a few weeks after he has looked at the team's books, talked with Huizenga, and has a better idea of whether the deal will go through.

Chikovsky said that if the group purchased the franchise, they would not move the team north of south Palm Beach County but might consider proposals from Broward's competitors. Dade and Palm Beach officials have talked about building a new home for the Panthers outside the Miami Arena, but nothing concrete has emerged.

"We want the Panthers in Broward because we've been told that that's the best place for them to be," said Chikovsky. "But if Dade or Palm Beach wanted to talk, I'd be happy to listen."

Attorneys who have tried cases with the pair say it is Chikovsky, not Shapiro, who has the major interest in sports. But they add that Shapiro is a determined man who often gets what he wants.

Shapiro and Chikovsky say they want assurances from Huizenga that he'll keep his promise to donate $25 million to Broward County toward construction of an arena if a local buyer comes forward by Feb. 1.

Shapiro hopes he has a leg up on the out-of-town offers because Huizenga has promised publicly that he prefers to sell to someone who will keep the Panthers in the area.

"That's why I'm willing to go through with the offer," said Shapiro. "If he's a man of his word, then I'll own the team."

Meanwhile, Broward County commissioners on Tuesday moved a step closer to meeting Huizenga's Feb. 1 deadline for putting together a financing deal for the $165 million arena. But they aren't happy about Huizenga's deadlines. Shapiro said he need three to four months to close the deal.

County commissioners also have questions for the team. One key point: Huizenga had offered in the past to cover cost overruns or make rent payments on the arena for up to $1 million a year over 30 years. Shapiro didn't say whether he'd be willing to do any of that.

Commissioners were anxious at Tuesday's morning meeting to see a prospective owner emerge before they promised to build an arena. But they did agree Tuesday to hire a consulting firm to study possible sites in Fort Lauderdale and Sunrise, and develop a financing plan. The firm has until Jan. 24 to present commissioners with its findings.

The commission will hold a special meeting on Jan. 30 to consider the plan.

Herald staff writers Cindy Goodman and Connie Prater contributed to this report.

Rochester *Democrat and Chronicle*, April 3, 1996

Land donated to YMCA

'Tangible' site helps push Wayne's plans

by Doris Wolf, staff writer

First it was an idea, then it was a schedule of programs. Now the Western Wayne YMCA is a field of dreams.

James Shapiro of the Rochester law firm Shapiro & Shapiro has donated 86.5 acres on a hillside near the Walworth town office building to the Greater Rochester YMCA.

It will be the site of a new YMCA in Wayne County. The transfer of the land was completed at the end of 1995, said town officials.

"All my life, I have tried to help the silent victim," Shapiro said in explaining his decision to make the donation. "I just really feel for people who don't have a lot of money. It is easy for people who have funds to go to a country club or buy exercise equipment. But people who aren't rich deserve to have an opportunity, too. The YMCA has a more than 140-year history of helping people."

Supervisor Peg Churchill said the property, which Shapiro valued at $823,000, will be surveyed and a feasibility and marketing study will get under way soon.

Shapiro said he hopes the donation will allow the town and the YMCA to get a jump start on its goal to construct a facility by 2002.

Town code enforcement officer John Aman said the donated land is "an interesting piece of property, with woodlands, a ravine and nicely tiered areas." The land backs up to about 60 acres of town-owned land on Daansen Road which had been used as a gravel pit. The additional acreage could be used for future expansion, Churchill said.

She said the gift gives western Wayne County people "something tangible and will help to establish a goal to develop a Y."

"When people are asked how to improve Walworth, recreational facilities are frequently mentioned," Churchill said.

Early last year, she joined the board of the Southeast Y to help the group build a bridge to Wayne County. The Southeast Y used its own funds and staff to help establish a Y Without Walls. It hoped to conduct programs that would build local support for the organization before a major fund-raising effort is undertaken.

That's why last summer the Southeast YMCA offered a swimming program at the Gananda pool and a summer day camp for children. Churchill said results were mixed and a bit disappointing.

Rick Hopkins, executive director of the Southeast Y, said the cautious response was understandable: "It will take a couple of years to convince people we are for real," he said.

Rochester *Democrat and Chronicle*, September 21, 1996

Women sue Norplant

Area consumers among those claiming bad reactions

by Michael Zeigler, staff writer

Joanne Boutte was using a Norplant contraceptive implant for only a few days when she began to suffer headaches and dizziness.

The symptoms worsened and within six months she was transformed from an upbeat, confident medical billing clerk to an uptight, depressed and forgetful woman who couldn't work and always seemed on the verge of hysteria.

"It's been quite devastating," said Boutte, who lives in the Town of Greece with her husband and three children. "I couldn't focus. I couldn't think. At times I felt like I was losing my mind."

Now Boutte, 34, has joined 1,400 other women in New York—including 965 in the western section—to sue Norplant's manufacturer, Wyeth-Ayerst Laboratories of Philadelphia.

In personal-product liability lawsuits filed this week in U.S. District Court in Rochester and Buffalo, the women claim they have suffered severe side effects from using the contraceptive.

They allege Norplant has caused irregular or prolonged menstrual periods, headaches, nervousness, nausea, dizziness, dermatitis, acne, weight gain, change in appetite, numbness and pain at the implantation site and in the arm or hand, and enlargement of the ovaries or fallopian tubes.

Rochester attorney James J. Shapiro, who represents the women, maintains Wyeth put the product on the market even though it knew of harmful side effects.

He also alleges the product is deliberately marketed mostly to low-income women.

"If this was sold to rich people or middle-class people, it would never have been approved," he said.

Although Wyeth acknowledges some potential side effects, such as irregular menstrual bleeding, headaches, nausea, dizziness, nervousness and removal difficulties, it disputes claims that Norplant is unsafe.

"We still stand by the safety and efficacy of the product and we'll continue to fight the lawsuits aggressively," said Wyeth spokesman Audrey Ashby.

She also noted that the federal Food and Drug Administration reaffirmed its support for Norplant in August 1995, saying it found "no basis for questioning the safety and effectiveness" of the contraceptive.

The women suing in New York aren't asking for specific amounts of money for damages in their lawsuits, which involve the greatest number of plaintiffs in federal actions filed in Western New York in recent memory.

Although the lawsuits are the first filed against Norplant locally, numerous women across the nation have made similar claims in nearly 300 lawsuits.

But federal judges in Illinois and Texas have rejected efforts to allow lawsuits there to be certified as class-action suits, which would make benefits from potential settlements available to any women who used Norplant.

Rochester primary care physician Dr. Eric Schaff, who has implanted Norplant in more than 400 women, said he stands by it.

"There are many women who are very happy with it," he said.

Norplant was introduced in the United States in 1991, after two decades of tests in 55 nations. Nearly 1 million American women—and about 3 million worldwide—have used it.

Boutte used Norplant from January to June 1992 after reading about extensive tests that were performed on the contraceptive.

"I figured if it had been tested for that many years, and went through the approval of the Food and Drug Administration, it must be safe," she said.

Crystal Alexander of Rochester used Norplant from 1991 to 1993. Although the symptoms she attributes to Norplant weren't as severe as Boutte's, she believes her problems were caused by the contraceptive and has also filed a lawsuit.

"I really wanted to get my tubes tied but my doctor talked me out of it and suggested the Norplant," said Alexander, 33, a mother of three.

She suffered from headaches and acne, and her menstrual period, normally lasting three days a month, began coming twice a month and lasted seven days.

She had the implants removed when she decided they were the cause of her problems.

Alexander and Boutte retained Shapiro after he ran a series of television ads inviting women to contact him if they had used Norplant and suffered from unexplained medical problems.

Syracuse Herald-Journal, December 16, 1996

Annoyed viewers find they can't nail ads by 'The Hammer'

By Dick Case

Joe Hall's sick of getting hammered by "The Hammer."

The Syracusan tells me he's had it up to here with the machine-gun, take-no-prisoners style of a lawyer named Jim Shapiro, who appears in his own TV commercials on local stations.

Jim calls himself "The Hammer."

He also, in his news releases, calls himself a "celebrity personal injury lawyer," "the meanest, nastiest S.O.B. in town" and "the notoriously aggressive Hundred Million Dollar Super-Lawyer."

Joe calls The Hammer "extremely offensive. I believe in freedom of expression, but this is in extremely bad taste."

Joe got in touch with Syracuse stations that broadcast the commercials. He was told other complaints had been received but on review, the ads passed muster.

This TV watcher isn't satisfied.

"It's too bad we don't have an opportunity to complain, except to the TV stations," Joe continued. "I'm tired of being bombarded."

If Joe were a lawyer, he'd have another place to go, the grievance process. Jim has licenses in New York and Florida. He's a partner in Shapiro and Shapiro of Rochester. His father, Sidney, is the other Shapiro on the shingle.

"They came after me for the ads." The Hammer said from his Rochester office the other day. "The 'old boy' network that doesn't advertise hates competition; they've been trying to silence me for years. I'm not going to be silenced."

He wasn't, at least by the state Supreme Court Appellate Division that recently considered a Grievance Committee complaint from fellow lawyers. The judges found his commercials "offensive" but constitutionally protected.

"Truthful, free speech will not be muzzled because a few rich lawyers are offended," Jim commented in a news release he faxed to me last week.

A court ruling 20 years ago allowed lawyers to advertise, although few went at it the way the Shapiros did. Jim's been hammering the tubes in Rochester since 1986 and the last seven years in Syracuse. The firm also buys time across New York and Florida (it has an office in Hollywood) for what Jim called "special torts."

I asked the lawyer about his TV persona, which seemed different from the softly spoken citizen I heard on the telephone.

Jim needs to hammer in the language of the streets, he explained, because he wants to reach folks on the street, "construction workers, busboys and other people who don't know they have the right to file claims.

"I'm very aggressive because I want to reach them in a way they understand."

The ads include snappy visuals and words flashing on the screen: "broken bones," "scars," " burns," "paralysis." Jim appears with his shirt unbuttoned, tie askew.

And the spinning hammer, of course. It seems to take the form of a judge's gavel.

The ads, which Jim said air "every day in Rochester and Syracuse," carry a toll-free number, which answers in Rochester. Potential clients in the Syracuse area are referred to an office in the University Building, where he said the firm has a staff of lawyers and paralegals.

When I told him about Joe Hall's complaint, Jim said he understood "some people hate me. That's OK. All they have to do is turn me off."

A footnote: The Shapiro and Shapiro news release mentioned a commemorative T-Shirt he has for sale, "featuring a vicious beast with blood dripping from its fangs and the legend Protected by Vicious S.O.B., Jim The Hammer Shapiro."

They go for $9.95, with profits to the Rochester YMCA.

COMPUTER KEYBOARDS

Computers and keyboards are a common feature in most work places and many homes. Yet these commonly used items may carry hidden dangers and potential for injury.

Some keyboards have been associated with repetitive stress injuries, including carpal tunnel syndrome and tendonitis. Such injuries can occur if a keyboard being used over a long term basis is not properly designed to prevent injury.

Several computer keyboard manufacturers have withheld information that would have allowed users to help avoid repetitive stress injuries The manufacturers made this information available to their own employees, but failed to disclose it to the general public, including purchasers of their products

If you have sustained a repetitive stress injury or other medical problems due to your use of a computer or keyboard, it is likely that you it is can bring a claim for workers' compensation. In addition to a workers' compensation claim, you may also be able to pursue a lawsuit against the keyboard or computer manufacturer. Consultation with an attorney may help to clarify your rights.

Information that may assist an attorney in assessing your claim includes the name of the manufacturer, model number of the keyboard that you use, length of time that you used this particular keyboard, how much training you received in use of the keyboard, whether any safety information was provided to you, how many hours of your workday were spent on the keyboard, and whether you have lost any earnings due to your injuries.

Other injuries may also be associated with poorly designed keyboards, computer stations, or work spaces. Such injuries include strain to the neck and back, and damage to vision. It has also been suggested that computers, as electronic devices that emit electromagnetic fields, may cause or contribute to certain cancers, birth defects, and other medical problems. If you have sustained such injuries due to defects in the design of a computer, keyboard, or work station, you may likewise wish to seek legal advice.

OTHER TOXIC EXPOSURES

Other products that have been shown to be toxic or otherwise dangerous include DES (a drug that was given to women in order to prevent miscarriages, which has been linked to cancer in the daughters and granddaughters of the women who took it); exposure to various chemicals; and vaccines that cause severe reactions. This list provides but a few examples of other toxic exposures. If you believe that you have sustained exposure to a toxic substance and have been injured as a result, you should not hesitate to investigate your legal rights. As previously discussed, failure to timely commence legal action may bar any right you have to recover. Further, as a practical matter, failure to document your injuries and the circumstances leading to those injuries as soon as possible after the exposure occurs, may significantly weaken your case.

SECTION FOUR

MEDICAL MALPRACTICE

Medical malpractice occurs when a doctor or other medical professional fails to conduct his or her practice in accord with reasonable care, thereby causing injury to a patient. Each aspect of this definition must be proved before a medical professional may be held liable for malpractice. For example, even if a doctor exercises reasonable care, he or she may be unable to save the life of a gravely ill or injured patient. The fact that the patient dies will not make the doctor liable for malpractice, because the doctor exercised reasonable care in treating the patient. Situations that could give rise to a medical malpractice claim, however, include:

—failure to diagnose—for example, if a patient repeatedly complains of symptoms that are commonly associated with cancer, yet the doctor fails to investigate such symptoms, and the patient later dies of cancer.

—failure to obtain informed consent—for example, if a patient is scheduled for cosmetic surgery in which one of the risks is excessive scarring, but the doctor does not explain such risk and obtain the patient's consent to that risk, and the patient is left with excessive scarring after the surgery.

—performing a surgical procedure on the wrong patient, or on the wrong part of a patient's body.

—leaving a surgical instrument inside of a patient's body.

In most medical malpractice claims, the patient's medical history and relationship with the medical professional are scrutinized by the opposing lawyer. While communications between doctors and their patients are ordinarily confidential, such confidentiality may be lifted once a lawsuit is commenced.

Proving that a medical professional has committed malpractice may be difficult. The only people qualified to determine whether malpractice has occurred are other doctors. A doctor who is called upon to testify may sympathize with the medical professional against whom the case is being brought. Such a doctor may present testimony that is unfavorable to the injured person.

No one wants to feel that they have been harmed by their doctor. You can help to avoid such feelings by selecting a doctor who regularly handles your type of medical problem. Provide the doctor an accurate and complete medical history, including information about any allergies, prior problems, current symptoms, and medications you take. Attend all exams, treatments, and referrals scheduled by your doctor. Notify your doctor immediately if you have side effects from any medicine prescribed for you, or if you get worse for any reason.

The doctor needs complete information to properly diagnose and treat you. Information that you regard as unimportant may be critical to your care. Only your doctor can decide what information is important.

If your doctor advises you to undergo surgery or if you have questions about your doctor's treatment plan for a serious condition, you may wish to seek a second opinion. Getting a second opinion is not disrespectful to your doctor. Second opinions are so important that many health insurance policies require that a second opinion be obtained before surgery is performed.

SECTION FIVE

STOCKBROKER MISCONDUCT

IS YOUR STOCKBROKER ON YOUR SIDE?

Stockbrokers are salespeople. Stockbrokers generally work for brokerage firms, which make commissions when an investor buys or sells securities. The brokerage firm pays the stockbroker a percentage of the firm's commission on the transaction. The more transactions that a particular broker handles, the more commissions that are generated for the brokerage firm and thus for the individual broker. While brokers want investors to use their services, they sometimes do not keep track of how much profit an individual investor makes.

The goals of the brokerage firm (large commissions) and the goal of the investors (income and appreciation) have little common ground. When an investment yields a large return to the investor, the broker does not earn any additional commission. The broker's earnings are based on the volume of business that he or she generates for the brokerage firm. Therefore, the broker has a disincentive for making a sale from which the investor will reap large profits.

Where the brokerage firm offers large commissions for selling particular securities, brokers have an incentive to sell those securities to investors. But ironically, payment of a large commission to the broker lowers the chance of the investor earning a profit. For example, sales of limited partnerships can earn the broker very large commissions. The broker may be pushed by the brokerage firm to sell as much of these high commission products as possible. Often these limited partnerships are very poor investments because the investor receives a low return (yield), has no liquidity, and runs a very high risk of losing the invested money.

The unlucky investor can be subjected to much worse than inflated commissions. An unethical broker may want more than a substantial commission on the investor's account. Such a broker may try to make extra commissions by violating the rules of the NASD (National Association of Securities Dealers) as follows:

1. Churning-Excessively trading an account just to earn commissions.

2. Unsuitable investments—Investing money in an investment not appropriate for the investor.

3. Unauthorized trading—Buying and selling securities without the investor's permission.

4. Promises not delivered—Making promises or telling half truths so that the investor will buy an investment that he or she would otherwise not buy.

Victims of stockbrokers' misconduct can fight back. Arbitration or litigation are methods by which investors who have lost money due to improper conduct by their brokers can seek to recover their losses. Federal and State laws prohibit brokers from misrepresenting investments, omitting important information about the risks associated with particular investments and recommending securities that are unsuitable for the investor. Other actionable complaints include unauthorized trading, excessive trading and failure to carry out an investor's orders.

WHAT IS UNSUITABILITY?

Unsuitable investments are those that are not appropriate for the investor's financial needs and circumstances.

When an investor opens an account with a stockbroker, the stockbroker asks questions about the investor's income, net worth, liquid net worth (cash available to invest), age, investment goals and occupation. The stockbroker needs this information to determine whether an investment is suitable for the investor's financial situation. Stockbrokers have an obligation to recommend only suitable investments.

For example, an eighty year old retiree should not invest all of his or her money in one limited partnership investment involving oil and gas, for a number of reasons:

1. No investor should place all of his or her money into one investment. If the investment fails, the investor has no money left.

2. A limited partnership is an investment for the future—perhaps 20 years from now. It is not suitable for an elderly investor, who will probably not live to receive his or her money back.

3. An investment in oil and gas is often a high risk investment. Older investors generally cannot afford the risk associated with such investments.

4. An elderly investor may need income to pay bills. An oil and gas investment does not have a reliable income stream.

5. Most oil and gas limited partnerships are not traded on an open market. If the investor needed money, the investment could not be sold to raise cash.

WHAT IS CHURNING?

Churning occurs when brokers encourage investors to needlessly buy and sell often, in order to generate more commissions.

Stockbrokers make money by getting a commission every time investors buy or sell securities. The more often a broker buys and sells on an investor's behalf, the more commissions the broker can earn.

It is often easy to tell that an account has been churned. If commissions paid to the broker exceed any reasonable amount of profit the investments could have made, the account has probably been oversold.

Investments are usually made for the long term. It is almost impossible for an investor to profit from frequent sales of stock, since the commissions will exceed any profit made. Only the broker comes out ahead when an account is churned.

WHY ARE SOME MUNICIPAL BONDS UNSAFE INVESTMENTS?

Brokers have convinced many investors that municipal bonds are a safe, secure and reliable investment. Brokers may assure investors that they will receive a fair return (interest) on the investment and have the security of a state or local government to pay back the bond.

However, the broker may not tell the investor that:

1. There may be a large spread between the buy price and sell price. This price difference represents the broker's commission. The commission can be between 1/2% to 4% of the total amount invested. Most investors <u>never</u> <u>know</u> <u>the</u> <u>commission</u> received by their broker on a municipal bond purchase or sale.

   Brokers often have discretion to mark-up or mark-down the bonds depending on what price they think the investor will pay (where the investor is buying bonds) or accept (where the investor is selling bonds). This discretionary mark-up or mark-down can change the amount of the broker's commission, and the amount that the investor pays for the bond or receives from the bond's sale.

2. Not all bonds are safe and secure. Municipal bonds are only as safe as the government authority that issues them. High yield bonds can be risky investments.

3. If interest rates go up, the investor may be stuck with the low paying bonds. If interest rates go down, the high rate may not be locked in. The issuer of the bond can often "call" bonds and re-borrow the money at a

lower rate. In such circumstances, the investor bears all of the risks of interest rate changes.

WHAT ARE WRAP ACCOUNTS?

Wrap accounts provide financial advice in exchange for a fixed annual fee. Investors are offered professional money management for a fraction of the investment normally required to get such expert advice. The investor is told that the brokerage firm can offer these services by pooling many small investors together. But such promises are frequently too good to be true.

Wrap accounts often come with large annual fees—sometimes up to 5% of the assets in the account. Yet the investor may be unaware of the hidden charges that are part of the wrap fee.

An investor who purchases a wrap account is paying one manager to manage the stocks and bonds in the portfolio, and a second manager—usually the brokerage firm—to manage the manager. Such management fees may be taken as a fee, or directly out of the assets of the fund.

Further, the wrap fee must cover a profit for the investor's own broker. By adding layer after layer of managers and brokers, the investor's "one-time" annual fee is so high that an unrealistic profit is needed to just break even.

Any trades that the investor executes may also carry fees, which are generally not included in the wrap fee. Most funds must execute their trades through the brokerage house that sends the business to them. This prevents the fund manager from obtaining the best price on a trade.

Brokers love to sell wrap accounts, because such accounts guarantee a commission on the investor's account for the whole year and require little to no work by the broker.

In summary, the broker may neglect to tell the wrap investor that:

1. The broker receives a large yearly payment just for selling a wrap investment;

2. The brokerage firm charges a large fee for picking out the "best" money manager;

3. The money manager also gets paid for overseeing your investment;

4. All trades may be required to be made through the brokerage firm that recommended the wrap account. No competition exists to lower the commissions or spreads. Even worse, since the money cannot be spread over many brokerage firms, the price of the investment could be severely hurt by the large size of the trade.

ARBITRATION

What is arbitration?

When an investor opens a new account at a brokerage firm, the investor must sign an agreement that governs the investor's rights in the event of a dispute with the firm. In most cases, the investor agrees that disputes will be resolved by arbitration rather than through a lawsuit in court.

Arbitration is an alternative to the courts to resolve disputes. The goal of arbitration is to resolve disputes quickly, inexpensively, and fairly.

The dispute is referred to one or more impartial persons who act as arbitrators. The arbitrators hear all of the evidence relating to the dispute, and then make a final and binding determination. Arbitration is private and informal.

The parties can agree in advance on certain arbitrators or can follow a procedure set up by an independent arbitration organization, such as the American Arbitration Association, to select the arbitrators.

After the arbitrators are selected, the parties must prepare for the arbitration hearing. All communications and preparations for the arbitration hearing are conducted through the arbitration organization. The arbitrators are not informed of the parties' positions until the actual hearing. Therefore, it is unlikely that evidence or arguments will be given to the arbitrators without the other party having an opportunity to contest the argument or evidence.

The parties are responsible for assembling all documents and papers needed for the hearing. As part of this preparation, the investor can request documents from the stock-broker or brokerage firm. The investor should also obtain interviews of all of the witnesses before the arbitration. Parties can subpoena documents or witnesses. The parties should make sure arrangements are made to record the arbitration.

Each party has the right to be represented by a lawyer at the hearing. Each party can present their case to the arbitrators. In most claims, the party bringing the claim presents their side first. The legal procedures followed at arbitration hearings are similar to those used in court trials. The rules of evidence are not as strictly followed at arbitration as at trial.

Most arbitration hearings proceed in the following order:

First, there is a brief opening statement by each party. Next, the claimant tells the arbitrators the remedy sought. The claimant must explain how the remedy sought is within the arbitrators' authority. Next, the witnesses testify. Cross-examination is allowed. Finally, a closing statement is given by each party.

After both sides have presented their arguments, the arbitrators declare the hearing closed. In most cases, the arbitrators have 30 days to render a decision. A decision is called an "award" in arbitration. Most awards are binding on the parties and can not be appealed. The awards are usually enforceable in the civil courts, if not complied with by the parties.

Most arbitrations for securities claims must be heard by an association specified in the investor's agreement with brokerage firm. Most agreements require binding arbitration by the National Association of Securities Dealers (NASD) or the American Arbitration Association (AAA).

The main office of the NASD is 1735 K Street NW, Washington, DC 20006. Their phone number is (202) 728–8000. The NASD rules of arbitration are found in the NASD manual. Their rules for arbitration that they call the "Code of Arbitration Procedure" is found in Chapter 3701 through Chapter 3746 of the manual.

The American Arbitration Association has its main office at 1450 West 51st Street, New York, NY 10020. The AAA has 35 offices in major cities. The rules and procedures can be received by contacting the AAA at the above address.

What are the costs of arbitration?

The cost of going to arbitration can be high, sometimes exceeding $10,000.00. Arbitration costs can include attorney fees, expert witness fees, arbitrator fees, transcript costs and fees to the arbitration association responsible for the claim. Most of these costs must be paid in advance. Most of these costs must be paid even if the investor does not recover his or her losses. The costs are as follows:

1. Claim filing fee—This fee must be paid for filing the claim with the arbitration association. For example, the NASD charges $150.00 for disputes dealing with amounts up to $50,000.00 and $250.00 for disputes dealing with amounts up to $500,000.00 dispute. This charge is non-refundable and must be paid in advance.

2. Hearing session deposit—At the time of filing a claim, the NASD also requires a hearing session deposit. A hearing session is any meeting between the parties and the arbitrators. For a three arbitrator, $50,000.00 claim, the hearing deposit is $600.00. For a $500,000.00 claim, the deposit is $1,000.00.

3. Expert witness fee—Most cases require the use of an expert witness to prove investors' losses. Expert witnesses often charge between $2,000.00 and $8,000.00

depending on the complexity of the case and the time required to testify.

Securities lawyers can charge between $100.00 and $400.00 per hour. Securities cases often require extensive legal work. This could result in thousands of dollars of legal fees.

Some lawyers handle securities cases on a contingency fee basis, and will advance the costs associated with arbitration. An attorney who represents investors on a contingency fee basis will charge no fee unless money is recovered on the investor's behalf. The lawyer will take a percentage of any recovery as their fee. Naturally, a lawyer will not agree to these terms unless they are confident in the investor's case.

Should you go to arbitration or settle?

The brokerage firm may make an offer to settle without going to arbitration. The investor will then need to decide whether to accept the settlement offer or wait for a hearing.

The advantages of settling your claim include the following:

1. You know how much you will receive.

2. You will receive your money now rather than later.

3. You have no risk of losing and getting nothing for your claim.

4. You will not have to pay additional hearing costs and expert witness fees.

5. You will not be surprised by new information that could hurt or ruin your claim.

6. You can put the matter behind you and go on with your life.

7. You will not risk the chance that the broker or brokerage firm will run out of assets or declare bankruptcy before you win. It is useless to win if you cannot collect.

The disadvantages of settling your case include the following:

1. A settlement is final. You cannot re-open the case if new information is discovered.

2. The arbitrators could give much more money than the current settlement offer.

Many claims settle before arbitration. This is because the brokerage firms and claimants both know that arbitrators can give a large award, a small award, or no award at all. Arbitration can be expensive for both sides. A lawyer's time in court is worth thousands of dollars each day. Expert witnesses' fees can be immense. The total cost of going to arbitration, combined with the unknown outcome, often makes the decision easy.

In some cases, however, the offer made by the brokerage firm is not fair. Going to arbitration may be advantageous in these instances. A small offer means little risk if the case is submitted to arbitration.

You should consult with your lawyer and ask his or her advice on settling any claim. Law firms that handle securities claims will know the brokerage firm's tactics and will know whether a settlement offer is fair. Your lawyer will also be aware of the strengths and weaknesses of your case and will be able to advise you about the risks and benefits associated with settlement and arbitration.

You can win in arbitration even if you were at fault for the loss.

After you lose money in an investment, your friends and family may tell you that it was your own fault. You might think that you knew the risks of the investment and just had bad luck or made a poor investment decision.

You can make a claim against your broker and brokerage firm even if you think you knew and took the risks in the following situations:

1. The broker lied to you about the real risks.

2. The investment was unsuitable for your investment situation or stated goals.

3. The broker made untrue promises or misrepresented the investment.

4. The broker "churned" the account by encouraging you to frequently to buy and sell securities.

5. Too much of your investment portfolio was invested in one or two risky investments.

Investors who have sustained losses often think that they are responsible for such losses. Some investors may believe that their own greed caused the loss. Such investors should consider whether the broker created the greed by making promises of a substantial profit within a short amount of time.. If the broker made unrealistic promises in order to sell the investment, the broker's conduct may be actionable, notwithstanding the investor's desire for a large, fast profit. Only a lawyer experienced in securities litigation should determine if the loss was your fault or the broker's.

HOW TO USE INFORMATION ON YOUR BROKERAGE FORM TO SUPPORT YOUR CLAIM

When an investor opens a new account at a stock brokerage firm, he or she provides important information to the stockbroker. This information includes details about the investor's net worth, income, cash available to invest, investment goals, property ownership, age and marital status. The answers to these questions are very important, because they inform the broker of the risks that the investor can or cannot take.

In most cases investors learn about investments from their brokers. Since brokers are professionals, it is not unusual for investors to follow their broker's advice.

If a broker sells an investment that is not suitable for an investor's financial situation, the account form is the proof that the broker knew about the investor's finances. For example, a $30,000.00 investment in a risky limited partnership or in options might be an acceptable risk for a young doctor earning $350,000.00 per year, and having a liquid net worth of more than $1,000,000.00. This example assumes the doctor understands the risk.However, a similar $30,000.00 investment for a retired widow, living on Social Security with only a $50,000.00 net worth is not proper.

QUESTIONS YOUR LAWYER WILL ASK

When you first meet with your lawyer, you will be asked many questions. These questions are aimed at getting the information needed to investigate and prepare your claim. Your attorney cannot afford to be surprised later about an important piece of information. The following is a list of common questions asked by lawyers of their clients:

1. Name

2. Home address

3. Phone numbers at home and work

4. Age

5. Social Security Number

6. Marital Status

7. Spouse's name

8. Age of spouse

9. Children's names and ages

10. Occupation

11. List of all persons living in the household, their ages and if they are dependent on you

12. Name of any broker or brokerage firm to which you have made any complaints in writing or on the phone

13. Copies of any account documents you have

14. Copies of all documents received from the broker

15. Your net worth

16. Income received from the investment

17. Amount you invested with the broker, dates invested, and what types of investments made

18. Other investments that you have made and their results

19. Other brokers and brokerage firms with whom you have had accounts

20. Source of all income and amounts

21. Amount you lost

22. What was your financial situation when you made the investment(s)

23. What education and experience do you have with investing.

Your lawyer will probably ask more questions depending upon your specific case.

QUESTIONS TO ASK YOUR BROKER BEFORE YOU MAKE ANY INVESTMENT

It is important to learn about any investment before making a purchase. The following are typical questions that your broker should be able to answer:

1. How much of your money is actually going into the investment? How much of your initial investment goes for commissions, markups of the securities, expenses of the offer, and other related expenses?

2. How much is charged each year by the managers of the investment to manage your money?

3. How much are you charged by the owners or partners to oversee the managers each year?

4. What kind of market exists to sell your investment? Unless a large exchange exists to list and sell your investment you may suffer a large loss if you want to sell out.

5. How is the return of your investment guaranteed?

6. Is this investment suitable for someone your age, with your income, with your net worth, and with your investment goals?

7. What are the risks of this type of investment?

8. What are the tax aspects of your investment?

9. What prior track record exists for the same type of investment?

10. What rate of return can you expect on your money?

11. When can you expect to receive back your investment and from what source?

12. Are there any documents that you can read from the seller or sponsor of the investment?

13. Are there any published articles or other information available about the investment from sources other than the investment's sponsor?

14. Can you afford to lose the money you are investing?

15. Do you need the money for an emergency or unexpected expense in the near future?

16. Are you well diversified into different low risk investments?

Always ask your broker to put answers to your questions in writing. Then you will have proof of your broker's claims and promises.

IMPORTANT NAMES, ADDRESSES, AND PHONE NUMBERS

Most arbitrations are with the NASD or American Arbitration Association. Their main offices are listed below:

NASD (National Association of Securities Dealers)
1735 K Street NW
Washington, DC 20006
Telephone No.: 202-728-8000

American Arbitration Association
140 West 51st St
New York, NY 10020
Telephone No.: 212-484-4000
Facsimile No.: 212-765-4874

New York Stock Exchange, Inc.
Constitution and Rules can be purchased from:
Commerce Clearing House, Inc.
4025 West Peterson Ave
Chicago, Illinois 60646
Phone No.: 1-800-248-3248

Arbitration Journal
Published quarterly by American Arbitration Association
Subscriptions write to:
Hilda Melendez
American Arbitration Association
140 West 51st St
New York, NY 10020

Arbitration Times
Also published by American Arbitration Association
See address above or call 1-212-484-4000

New York Stock Exchange
11 Wall St.
New York, NY 10005

SECURITIES ARBITRATION RULES OF THE AMERICAN ARBITRATION ASSOCIATION

AS AMENDED AND EFFECTIVE ON MAY 1, 1993.

Introduction

Each year, millions of transactions involving security and commodity futures take place. Occasionally, disagreements develop over these transactions. Many of these disputes are resolved by arbitration, the voluntary submission of a dispute to a disinterested person or persons for final and binding determination. Arbitration has proven to be an effective way to resolve these disputes privately, promptly and economically.

The American Arbitration Association (AAA) is a public-service, not-for-profit organization offering a broad range of dispute-resolution services to business executives, attorneys, individuals, trade associations, unions, management, consumers, families, communities and all levels of government. Services are available through AAA headquarters in New York City and through offices located in major cities throughout the United States. Hearings may be held at locations convenient for the parties and are not limited to cities with AAA offices. In addition, the AAA serves as a center for education and training, issues specialized publications, and conducts research on all forms of out-of-court dispute settlement.

In October of 1991, the American Arbitration Association created a Securities Arbitration Task Force, comprised of representatives of various brokerage firms, customers' attorneys and others with considerable knowledge and experience in securities matters and the arbitration process. The mission of the Task Force was to consider improvements in the AAA's Securities Arbitration Rules and administrative procedures and policies that would make AAA-administered arbitration more attractive to all participants in the process. An effort was made at the same time to consider changes that would make the Securities Arbitration Rules applicable to commodity futures matters. The task force met 11 times from November 1991 through February 1993.

The report of the task force was endorsed by the AAA's Practice Committee and the rules are amended effective May 1, 1993 in response to the report.

An expedited system has been included in the rules for cases in which each party's claims involve less than $25,000, exclusive of interest and arbitration costs. This will assist parties in resolving such claims.

The rules contain procedures for the selection of arbitrators with appropriate expertise, including both those affiliated with the securities industry and those who are not. In the interest of fairness, the AAA has developed specific guidelines defining what constitutes an industry-affiliated arbitrator. Under these rules, lists of arbitrators and biographical information on each are sent to the parties for selection of the arbitrators.

In addition, the arbitrators sign an oath of office and are required to disclose any relationship with the parties or their representative even if such circumstances become known after the heating commences.

These features, as well as others contained in the rules, will assist the parties in resolving disputes fairly and promptly.

Governmental agencies have issued guidelines and regulations governing arbitration of future disputes involving securities. Consistent with such regulations, the parties can provide for the arbitration of future disputes by inserting the following clause into their contracts.

Standard Arbitration Clause

Any controversy or claim arising out of or relating to this contract, or the breach thereof, shall be settled by arbitration administered by the American Arbitration Association under its Securities Arbitration Rules, and judgment on the award rendered by the arbitrator(s) may be entered in any court having jurisdiction thereof.

Arbitration of existing disputes may be accomplished by use of the following:

We, the undersigned parties, hereby agree to submit to arbitration administered by the American Arbitration Association under its Securities Arbitration Rules the following controversy: (cite briefly). We further agree that the above controversy be submitted to (one)(three) arbitrator(s). We further agree that we will faithfully observe this agreement and the rules, that we will abide by and perform any award rendered by the arbitrator(s), and that a judgment of the court having jurisdiction may be entered on the award.

The services of the AAA are generally concluded with the transmittal of the award. Although there is voluntary compliance with the majority of awards, judgment on the award can be entered in a court having appropriate jurisdiction if necessary.

Administrative Fees

The AAA's administrative fees are based on service charges. There is a filing fee based on the amount of the claim or counterclaim, ranging from $300 on claims below $25,000 to a maximum of $4,000 for claims in excess of $5 million. In addition, there are service charges for hearings held and postponements and a processing fee for prolonged cases. This fee information allows the parties to exercise control over their administrative fees. The fees cover AAA administrative services; they do not cover arbitrator compensation or expenses, reporting services, or any post award charge incurred by the parties in enforcing the award.

Mediation

The parties may wish to submit their dispute to mediation prior to arbitration. In mediation, the neutral mediator assists the parties in reaching a settlement, but does not have the authority to make a binding decision or award. Mediation is administered by the AAA in accordance with its Commercial Mediation Rules. There is no additional administrative fee where parties to a pending arbitration attempt to mediate their dispute under the AAA's auspices.

If the parties want to adopt mediation as a part of their contractual dispute settlement procedure, they can insert the following mediation clause into their contract in conjunction with a standard arbitration provision.

> If a dispute arises out of or relates to this contract, or the breach thereof and if the dispute cannot be settled through negotiation, the parties agree first to try in good faith to settle the dispute by mediation administered by the American Arbitration Association and its Commercial Mediation Rules before resorting to arbitration, litigation, or some other dispute resolution procedure.

If the parties want to use a mediator to resolve an existing dispute, they can enter into the following submission.

> The parties hereby submit the following dispute to mediation administered by the American Arbitration Association under its Commercial Mediation Rules (the clause may also provide for the qualifications of the mediator(s), the method of payment, the locale of meetings and any other item of concern to the parties).

Even if your contract does not provide for administration by the AAA, arbitration or mediation might be available through pilot projects involving various brokerage firms and securities exchanges. Your local AAA office can provide more information about these programs.

Large Case Procedures

Recognizing that large, complex arbitrations often present unique procedural problems, the AAA, working with attorneys, arbitrators and industry advisory groups, has developed special Supplementary Procedures for Large, Complex Disputes as part of its Large, Complex Case Dispute Resolution Program. The overall purpose of these procedures is to provide for the efficient, economical and speedy resolution of larger disputes (i.e., cases involving claims in excess of $1,000,000). Cases are administered by senior AAA staff. The procedures provide for an early administrative conference with the AAA and a preliminary hearing with the arbitrators. Documentary exchanges and other essential exchanges of information are facilitated. The procedures also provide that a statement of reasons may accompany the award, if requested by the parties. The procedures are meant to supplement applicable rules that the parties have agreed to use. They include the possibility of the use of mediation to resolve some or all issues at an early stage.

The procedures are party driven. They will apply only where the parties agree to their use (unless a court or another entity directs their application) and the parties are free to modify any provision of the procedures. Indeed, the entire process may be tailored to suit the particular requirements of the parties to any single dispute.

Securities Arbitration Rules

1. Agreement of Parties

The parties shall be deemed to have made these rules a part of their arbitration agreement whenever they have provided for arbitration by the American Arbitration Association (hereinafter AAA) or under its Securities Arbitration Rules. These rules and any amendment of them shall apply in the form obtaining at the time the demand for arbitration or submission agreement involving a securities or commodity futures dispute is received by the AAA.

2. Name of Tribunal

Any tribunal constituted by the parties for the settlement of their dispute under these rules shall be called the Securities Arbitration Tribunal.

3. Administrator and Delegation of Duties

When parties agree to arbitrate under these rules, or when they provide for arbitration by the AAA and an arbitration is initiated under these rules, they thereby authorize the AAA to administer the arbitration. The authority and duties of the AAA are established in the agreement of the parties and in these rules, and may be carried out through such of the AAA's representatives as it may direct. The AAA may, in its discretion, assign the administration of an arbitration to any of its regional offices.

4. National Panel of Arbitrators

The AAA shall establish and maintain a National Panel of Securities Arbitrators and shall appoint arbitrators as provided in these rules.

5. Initiation under an Arbitration

Provision in a Contract

Arbitration under an arbitration provision in a contract shall be initiated in the following manner:

(a) The initiating party (hereinafter claimant) shall, within the time period, if any, specified in the contract(s), give written notice to the other party (hereinafter respondent) of its intention to arbitrate (demand), which notice shall contain a statement setting forth the nature of the dispute, the amount involved, if any, the remedy sought, and the hearing locale requested, and

(b) shall file at any regional office of the AAA three copies of the notice and three copies of the arbitration provisions of the contract, together with the appropriate filing fee as provided in the schedule. The AAA shall give notice of such filing to the respondent or respondents.

6. Answers and Third-Party Claims

A respondent may file an answering statement in duplicate with the AAA within 20 days from the commencement of administration, simultaneously sending a copy of the answering statement to the claimant. A party may also file an answer to a changed or new claim, as provided in Section 8. If no answering statement is filed within the time period stated above, it will be treated as a general denial of the claim.

If a counterclaim is asserted, it shall contain a statement setting forth the nature of the counterclaim, the amount involved, if any, and the remedy sought. If a counterclaim is made, the appropriate fee provided in the schedule shall be forwarded to the AAA with the answering statement.

If a respondent fails to file an answering statement within the time period stated above, the claimant may serve respondent with a written request for an answering statement. A respondent who fails to file an answer within 10 days of such a request may, in the discretion of the arbitrator, be barred from presenting any matter, argument or defense (other than a general denial) that could have been raised in an answering statement, but an arbitrator may not enter an award against a party without hearing evidence to support the making of an award. Arbitrators should endeavor to rule on requests to bar such matters prior to the hearing.

The demand or answer may assert a third-party claim against another party, if the third party is obliged to arbitrate the subject of that party's claim under these rules. The arbitrator is authorized to resolve any dispute over such joinder.

7. Initiation under a Submission

Parties to any existing dispute may start an arbitration under these rules by filing at any regional office of the AAA three copies of a written submission to arbitrate under these rules, signed by the parties. It shall contain a statement of the matter in dispute, the amount involved, if any, the remedy sought, and the hearing locale requested, together with the appropriate filing fee.

8. Changes of Claim

After filing of a claim, if either party desires to make any new or different claim or counterclaim, it shall be made in writing and filed with the AAA. Simultaneously, a copy must be sent to the other party, who shall have a period of 10 days from the date of such transmittal within which to file an answer with the AAA. After the arbitrator is appointed, however, no new or different claim may be submitted except with the arbitrator's consent.

9. Applicable Procedures

Unless the AAA in its discretion determines otherwise, the Expedited Procedures shall be applied in any case where no disclosed claim or counterclaim exceeds $25,000, exclusive of interest and arbitration costs. Parties may also agree to use the Expedited Procedures in cases involving claims in excess of $25,000. The Expedited Procedures shall be applied as described in Sections 51 through 55 of these rules, in addition to any other portion of these rules that is not in conflict with the Expedited Procedures.

All other cases shall be administered in accordance with Sections 1 through 50 of these rules.

10. Administrative Conference, Preliminary

Hearing and Mediation Conference

At the request of any party or at the discretion of the AAA, an administrative conference with the AAA and the parties and/or their representatives will be scheduled in appropriate cases to expedite the arbitration proceedings. There is no administrative fee for this service.

At the request of any party or at the discretion of the arbitrator or the AAA, a preliminary hearing with the parties and/or their representatives and the arbitrator may be scheduled by the arbitrator to specify issues to be resolved, to stipulate to uncontested facts, to schedule hearings to resolve the dispute, and to consider other matters that will expedite the arbitration proceedings. There is no administrative fee for the first preliminary hearing.

Unless the parties agree otherwise, the AAA at any stage of the proceeding may arrange a mediation conference under the Commercial Mediation Rules, in order to facilitate settlement. The mediator shall not be an arbitrator appointed to the case. Where the parties to a pending arbitration agree to mediate under the AAA's rules, no additional administrative fee is required to initiate the mediation.

11. Exchange of Information

Consistent with the expedited nature of arbitration, the arbitrator may establish (i) the extent of and schedule for production of documents and other information and (ii) identification of witnesses to be called. The arbitrator is authorized to resolve any dispute over this information exchange.

12. Fixing of Locale

The parties may agree on the locale where the arbitration is to be held. If any party requests that the hearing be held in a specific locale and the other party files no objection thereto within 20 days after notice of the request has been sent to it by the AAA, the locale shall be the one requested. If a party objects to the locale requested by the other party the AAA shall have the power to determine the locale and its decision shall be final and binding.

13. Qualifications of an Arbitrator

Any neutral arbitrator appointed pursuant to Section 14, 15, 16 or 52, or selected by mutual choice of the parties or their appointees, shall be subject to disqualification for the reasons specified in Section 20. If the parties agree in writing, the arbitrator shall not be subject to disqualification for those reasons.

Unless the parties agree otherwise, an arbitrator selected unilaterally by one party is a party-appointed arbitrator and is not subject to disqualification pursuant to Section 20.

The term "arbitrator" in these rules refers to the arbitration panel, whether composed of one or more arbitrators and whether the arbitrators are neutral or party appointed. An affiliated arbitrator is provided in Sections 14 and 18 is one who has or has had direct involvement in or relationship with the securities brokerage industry for a minimum of three years if now employed in that industry or for a minimum of five years if no longer so employed. Involvement in or relationship with would include (a) employment at a brokerage firm in a professional capacity, whether employed in sales, management, support or trading, or (b) employment as counsel, accountant or other professional who devotes a majority of his or her efforts to brokerage or brokerage-related matters. Persons out of the industry for more than 10 years are not affiliated. Persons whose firms or direct family members derive significant income from securities brokerage or brokerage-related matters, but who do not qualify as affiliated arbitrators as defined above, may not serve as arbitrators.

14. Appointment from Panel

If the parties have not appointed an arbitrator and have not provided any other method of appointment, the arbitrator shall be appointed in the following manner: immediately after the filing of the demand or submission, the AAA shall send simultaneously to each party to the dispute two lists of names and biographical information of persons chosen from the panel. The first list, from which one arbitrator will be appointed, will contain names of arbitrators affiliated with the securities industry. The second list, from which two arbitrators will be appointed, will contain names of arbitrators not affiliated with the securities industry. Additional biographical information on proposed arbitrators may be available from the AAA and will be furnished to a party upon request.

Each party to the dispute has 20 days from the transmittal date in which to strike any names objected to, number the remaining names in order of preference, and return the list to the AAA. If a party does not return the list within the time specified, all persons shall be deemed acceptable. From among the persons who have been approved on both lists and in accordance with the designated order of mutual preference, the AAA shall invite the arbitrator(s) who will serve.

If appointments cannot be made from the submitted list, the AAA will submit to the parties a final list of proposed arbitrators, consisting of a limited number of names. Each separately appearing party may strike on a peremptory basis one name for each arbitrator to be appointed, and return the list to the AAA within 10 days from the date of the AAA's transmittal to the parties. The AAA shall make the appointment(s) from the name(s) remaining on the list.

15. Direct Appointment by a Party

If the agreement of the parties names an arbitrator or specifies a method of appointing an arbitrator, that designation or method shall be followed. The notice of appointment, with the name and address of the arbitrator, shall be filed with the AAA by the appointing party. Upon the request of any appointing party the AAA shall submit a list of members of the panel from which the party may, if it so desires, make the appointment.

If the agreement specifies a period of time within which an arbitrator shall be appointed and any party fails to make the appointment within that period, the AAA shall make the appointment.

If no period of time is specified in the agreement, the AAA shall notify the party to make the appointment. If, within 20 days, an arbitrator has not been appointed by a party within the specified period, the AAA shall make the appointment.

16. Appointment of Neutral Arbitrator by Party-Appointed Arbitrators or Parties

If the parties have selected party-appointed arbitrators, or if such arbitrators have been appointed as provided in Section 15, and the parties have authorized them to appoint a neutral arbitrator within a specified time and no appointment is made within that time or any agreed extension, the AAA may appoint a neutral arbitrator, who shall act as chairperson.

If no period of time is specified for appointment of the neutral arbitrator and the party-appointed arbitrators or the parties do not make the appointment within 10 days from the date of the appointment of the last party-appointed arbitrator, the AAA may appoint the neutral arbitrator, who shall act as chairperson.

If the parties have agreed that their party-appointed arbitrators shall appoint the neutral arbitrator from the panel, the AAA shall furnish to the party-appointed arbitrators a list selected from the panel, and the appointment of the neutral arbitrator shall be made as provided in Section 14.

17. Nationality of Arbitrator in International Arbitration

Where the parties are nationals or residents of different countries, any neutral arbitrator shall, upon the request of any party, be appointed from among the nationals of a country other than that of any of the parties. The request must be made prior to the time set for the appointment of the arbitrator as agreed by the parties or set by these rules.

18. Number of Arbitrators

Where the claim of any party exceeds $25,000, the dispute shall be heard and determined by three arbitrators. Unless the parties otherwise agree, the majority shall be arbitrators not affiliated with the securities industry. All other disputes shall be heard and determined by one arbitrator not affiliated with the securities industry, as provided in Section 52.

19. Notice to Arbitrator of Appointment

Notice of the appointment of the neutral arbitrator, whether appointed by agreement of the parties or by the AAA, shall be sent to the arbitrator by the AAA, together with a copy of these rules. The signed acceptance of the arbitrator shall be filed with the AAA prior to the opening of the first hearing.

20. Disclosure and Challenge Procedure

Any person appointed as neutral arbitrator shall disclose to the AAA any circumstance likely to affect impartiality, including any bias or any financial or personal interest in the result of the arbitration or any past or present relationship with the parties or their representatives. Upon receipt of such information from the arbitrator or another source, the AAA shall communicate the information to the parties and, if it deems it appropriate to do so, to the arbitrator and others. Upon objection of a party to the continued service of a neutral arbitrator, the AAA shall determine whether the arbitrator should be disqualified and shall inform the parties of its decision, which shall be conclusive.

21. Vacancies

If for any reason an arbitrator is unable to perform the duties of the office, the AAA may, on proof satisfactory to it, declare the office vacant. Vacancies shall be filled in accordance with the applicable provisions of these rules.

In the event of a vacancy in a panel of arbitrators after the hearings have commenced, unless the parties agree otherwise, the vacancy shall be filled as provided above, and the newly constituted panel shall determine whether all or part of any prior hearing shall be repeated.

22. Date, Time and Place of Hearing

The arbitrator shall set the date, time and place for each hearing. The AAA shall send a notice of hearing to the parties at least 10 days in advance of the hearing date, unless otherwise agreed by the parties.

23. Representation

Any party may be represented by counsel or other authorized representative. A party intending to be represented shall notify the other party and the AAA of the name, address and telephone number of the representative at least three days prior to the date set for the hearing at which that person is first to appear. When a representative initiates an arbitration or responds for a party, notice of representation is deemed to have been given.

24. Stenographic Record

Any party desiring a stenographic record shall make arrangements directly with a stenographer and shall notify the other parties of these arrangements in advance of the hearing. The requesting party or parties shall pay the cost of the record, if the transcript is agreed by the parties to be, or determined by the arbitrator to be, the official record of the proceeding, it must be made available to the arbitrator and to the other parties for inspection, at a date, time and place determined by the arbitrator.

25. Interpreters

Any party wishing an interpreter shall make all arrangements directly with the interpreter and shall assume the costs of the service.

26. Attendance at Hearings; Experts

The arbitrator shall maintain the privacy of the hearings unless the law provides to the contrary. Any person having a direct interest in the arbitration is entitled to attend hearings. Although expert witnesses are generally permitted to attend the hearing, the arbitrator shall have the power to require the exclusion of any witness, other than a party or other essential person, during the testimony of any other witness. It shall be discretionary with the arbitrator to determine the propriety of the attendance of any other person.

27. Postponements

The arbitrator for good cause shown may postpone any hearing upon the request of a party or upon the arbitrator's own initiative, and shall grant a postponement when all of the parties agree.

28. Oaths

Before proceeding with the first hearing, each arbitrator may take an oath of office and, if required by law, shall do so. The arbitrator may require witnesses to testify under oath administered by any duly qualified person and, if it is required by law or requested by any party, shall do so.

29. Majority Decision

All decisions of the arbitrators must be by a majority. The award must also be made by a majority unless the concurrence of all is expressly required by the arbitration agreement or by law.

30. Order of Proceedings and Communication with Arbitrator

A hearing shall be opened by the filing of the oath of the arbitrator, where required; by the recording of the date, time and place of the hearing, and the presence of the arbitrator, the parties and their representatives, if any; and by the receipt by the arbitrator of the statement of the claim and the answering statement, if any.

The arbitrator may, at the beginning of the hearing, ask for statements clarifying the issues involved. In some cases, part or all of the above will have been accomplished at the preliminary hearing conducted by the arbitrator pursuant to Section 10.

The complaining party shall then present evidence to support its claim. The defending party shall then present evidence supporting its defense. Witnesses for each party shall submit to questions or other examination. The arbitrator has the discretion to vary this procedure but shall afford a full and equal opportunity to all parties for the presentation of any material and relevant evidence.

Exhibits, when offered by either party, may be received in evidence by the arbitrator.

The names and addresses of all witnesses and a description of the exhibits in the order received shall be made a part of the record.

There shall be no direct communication between the parties and a neutral arbitrator other than at oral hearing, unless the parties and the arbitrator agree otherwise. Any other oral or written communication from the parties to the neutral arbitrator shall be directed to the AAA for transmittal to the arbitrator.

31. Arbitration in the Absence of a Party or Representative

Unless the law provides to the contrary, the arbitration may proceed in the absence of any party or representative who, after due notice, fails to be present or fails to obtain a postponement. An award shall not be made solely on the default of a party. The arbitrator shall require the party who is present to submit such evidence as the arbitrator may require for the making of an award.

32. Evidence

The parties may offer evidence that is relevant and material to the dispute, and shall produce such evidence as the arbitrator deems necessary to an understanding and determination of the dispute. An arbitrator or other person authorized by law to subpoena witnesses or documents may do so upon the request of any party or independently.

The arbitrator shall be the judge of the relevance and materiality of the evidence offered, and conformity to legal rules of evidence shall not be necessary. All evidence shall be taken in the presence of all of the arbitrators and all of the parties, except where any of the parties is absent in default or has waived the right to be present.

33. Evidence by Affidavit and Post hearing Filing of Documents or Other Evidence

The arbitrator may receive and consider the evidence of witnesses by affidavit, but shall give it only such weight as the arbitrator deems it entitled to after consideration of any objection made to its admission.

If the parties agree or the arbitrator directs that documents or other evidence be submitted to the arbitrator after the hearing, the documents or other evidence shall be filed with the AAA for transmission to the arbitrator. All parties shall be afforded an opportunity to examine such documents or other evidence.

34. Inspection or Investigation

An arbitrator finding it necessary to make an inspection or investigation in connection with the arbitration shall direct the AAA to so advise the parties. The arbitrator shall set the date and time and the AAA shall notify the parties. Any party who so desires may be present at such an inspection or investigation. In the event that one or all parties are not present at the inspection or investigation, the arbitrator shall make a verbal or written report to the parties and afford them an opportunity to comment.

35. Interim Measures

The arbitrator may direct whatever interim measures are deemed necessary with respect to the dispute, including measures for the conservation of property, without prejudice to the rights of the parties or to the final determination of the dispute. Such interim measures may be taken in the form of an interim award and the arbitrator may require security for the costs of such measures.

36. Closing of Hearing

The arbitrator shall specifically inquire of all parties whether they have any further proofs to offer or witnesses to be heard. Upon receiving negative replies or if satisfied that the record is complete, the arbitrator shall declare the hearing closed.

If briefs are to be filed, the hearing shall be declared closed as of the final date set by the arbitrator for the receipt of briefs. If documents are to be filed as provided in Section 33 and the date set for their receipt is later than that set for the receipt of briefs, the later date shall be the date of closing the hearing. The time limit within which the arbitrator shall endeavor to make the award shall start to run, in the absence of other agreements by the parties, upon the closing of the hearing.

37. Reopening of Hearing

The hearing may be reopened on the arbitrator's initiative, or upon application of a party, at any time before the award is made. If reopening the hearing would prevent the making of the award within the specific time agreed on by the parties in the contract(s) out of which the controversy has arisen, the matter may not be reopened unless the parties agree on an extension of time. When no specific date is fixed in the contract, the arbitrator may reopen the hearing and shall have thirty days from the closing of the reopened hearing within which to make an award.

38. Waiver of Oral Hearing

Where each party's claim does not exceed $5,000, exclusive of interest and costs, the dispute shall be resolved by submission of documents, unless any party requests an oral hearing, or the arbitrator determines that an oral hearing is necessary. The parties may also provide, by written agreement, for the waiver of oral hearings in any case. If the parities are unable to agree as to the procedure, the AAA shall specify a fair and equitable procedure.

39. Waiver of Rules

Any party who proceeds with the arbitration after knowledge that any provision or requirement of these rules has not been complied with and who fails to state an objection in writing shall be deemed to have waived the right to object.

40. Extensions of Time

The parties may modify any period of time by mutual agreement. The AAA or the arbitrator may for good cause extend any period of time established by these rules, except the time for making the award. The AAA shall notify the parties of any extension.

41. Serving of Notice

Each party shall be deemed to have consented that any papers, notices, or process necessary or proper for the initiation or continuation of an arbitration under these rules; for any court action in connection therewith; or for the entry of judgment on any award made under these rules may be served on a party by mail addressed to the party or its representative at the last known address or by personal service, in or outside the state where the arbitration is to be held, provided that reasonable opportunity to be heard with regard thereto has been granted to the party.

The AAA and the parties may also use facsimile transmission, telex, telegram or other written forms of electronic communication to give the notices required by these rules.

42. The Award

(a) The arbitrator shall endeavor to issue the award promptly and, unless otherwise agreed by the parties, within 30 days from the date of closing of the hearing or, if oral hearings have been waived, from the date of the AAA's transmittal of the final statements and proofs to the arbitrator.

(b) The award shall be in writing, shall be signed by a majority of the arbitrators, and shall be executed in the manner required by law. The award shall contain the names of the parties and representatives, if any, a summary of the issues, including type(s) of any security or product in controversy, the damages and/or other relief requested and awarded, a statement of any other issues resolved, a statement regarding the disposition of any statutory claim, the names of arbitrators, the date when the case was filed, the date of the award, the number and dates of hearings, the location of the hearings, and the signatures of the arbitrators concurring in or dissenting from the award.

(c) The arbitrator may grant any remedy or relief that the arbitrator deems just and equitable and within the scope of the agreement of the parties, including, but not limited to, specific performance of a contract. The arbitrator shall, in the award, assess arbitration fees, expenses, and compensation as provided in Sections 46, 47 and 48 in favor of any party and, in the event that any administrative fees or expenses are due the AAA, in favor of the AAA.

(d) If the parties settle their dispute during the course of the arbitration, the arbitrator may, upon the written agreement of those parties, set forth the terms of the agreed settlement in an award. Such an award is called a consent award.

(e) Parties shall accept as legal delivery of the award the placing of the award or a true copy thereof in the mail addressed to a party or its representative at the last known address, personal service of the award, or the filing of the award in any other manner that is permitted by law.

(f) An award issued under these rules shall be publicly available provided that the names of the parties will not be publicly available.

43. Correction of Award

Within 20 days after the transmittal of an award, any party, upon notice to the other parties, may request that the arbitrator correct any clerical, typographical, technical or computational error in the award. The arbitrator is not empowered to redetermine the merits of any claim already decided.

The other parties shall be given 10 days to respond to the request. The arbitrator shall dispose of the request within 20 days after transmittal by the AAA to the arbitrator of the request and any response thereto.

44. Release of Documents for Judicial Proceedings

The AAA shall, upon the written request of a party, furnish to the party, at its expense, certified copies of any papers in the AAA's possession that may be required in judicial proceedings relating to the arbitration.

45. Applications to Court and Exclusion of Liability

(a) No judicial proceeding by a party relating to the subject matter of the arbitration shall be deemed a waiver of the party's right to arbitrate.

(b) Neither the AAA nor any arbitrator in a proceeding under these rules is a necessary party in judicial proceedings relating to the arbitration.

(c) Parties to these rules shall be deemed to have consented that judgment upon the arbitration award may be entered in any federal or state court having jurisdiction thereof.

(d) Neither the AAA nor any arbitrator shall be liable to any party for any act or omission in connection with any arbitration conducted under these rules.

46. Administrative Fees

As a not-for-profit organization, the AAA shall prescribe filing and other administrative fees to compensate it for the cost of providing administrative services. The fees in effect when the demand for arbitration or submission agreement is received shall be applicable.

The filing fee shall be advanced by the initiating party or parties, subject to final apportionment by the arbitrator in the award.

The AAA may, in the event of extreme hardship on the part of any party, defer or reduce the administrative fees.

47. Expenses

Unless the parties agree otherwise, all expenses of the arbitration, including required travel and other expenses of the arbitrator and AAA representatives, and the cost of any proof produced at the direct request of the arbitrator, shall be borne equally by the parties, subject to final allocation by the arbitrator as provided in Section 42(c).

48. Neutral Arbitrator's Compensation

Unless the parties agree otherwise, members of the National Panel of Securities Arbitrators will receive compensation for the first and second days of service at the rate of $400 per day per arbitrator, advanced equally by the parties.

For service thereafter, an appropriate daily rate and other arrangements will be discussed by the administrator with the parties prior to the appointment of the arbitrator. If the parties fall to agree to the terms of compensation, an appropriate rate will be established by the AAA and communicated in writing to the parties.

49. Deposits

The AAA may require the parties to deposit in advance of any hearings such sums of money as it deems necessary to cover the expense of the arbitration, including the arbitrator's fee, if any, and shall render an accounting to the parties and return any unexpended balance at the conclusion of the case.

50. Interpretation and Application of Rules

The arbitrator shall interpret and apply these rules in so far as they relate to the arbitrator's powers and duties. When there is more than one arbitrator and a difference arises among them concerning the meaning or application of these rules, it shall be decided by a majority vote. If that is not possible, either an arbitrator or a party may refer the question to the AAA for final decision. All other rules shall be interpreted and applied by the AAA.

51. Notice by Telephone

The parties shall accept all notices from the AAA by telephone. Such notices by the AAA shall subsequently be confirmed in writing to the parties. Should there be a failure to confirm in writing any notice hereunder, the proceeding shall nonetheless be valid if notice has, in fact, been given by telephone.

52. Appointment and Qualifications

The AAA shall submit simultaneously to each party an identical list of five proposed arbitrators drawn from the National Panel of Securities Arbitrators, from which one arbitrator shall be appointed. The arbitrators contained on the list will not be affiliated with the securities industry.

Each party may strike two names from the list on a peremptory basis. The list is returnable to the AAA within 20 days from the date of the AAA's transmittal to the parties.

If for any reason the appointment of an arbitrator cannot be made from the list, the AAA may make the appointment from among other members of the panel without the submission of additional lists.

The parties will be given notice by telephone by the AAA of the appointment of the arbitrator, who shall be subject to disqualification for the reasons specified in Section 20. Within seven days, the parties shall notify the AAA, by telephone, of any objection to the arbitrator appointed. Any objection by a party to the arbitrator shall be confirmed in writing to the AAA with a copy to the other party or parties.

53. Date, Time and Place of Hearing

The arbitrator shall set the date, time and place of the hearing. The AAA will notify the parties by telephone, at least seven days in advance of the hearing date. A formal notice of hearing will also be sent by the AAA to the parties.

54. The Hearing

Generally, the hearing shall be completed within one day, unless the dispute is resolved by submission of documents under Section 38. The arbitrator, for good cause shown, may schedule an additional hearing to be held within seven days.

55. Time of Award

Unless otherwise agreed by the parties, the arbitrator shall endeavor to render the award not later than 14 days from the date of the dosing of the hearing.

Administrative Fees

The AAA's administrative charges are based on filing and service fees. Arbitrator compensation, if any, is not included. Unless the parties agree otherwise, arbitrator compensation and administrative fees are subject to allocation by the arbitrator in the award.

Filing Fees

A non refundable filing fee is payable in full by a filing party when a claim, counterclaim, or additional claim is filed, as provided below.

Amount of Claim	Filing Fee
Up to $25,000	$300
Above $25,000 to $50,000	$500
Above $50,000 to $250,000	$1,000
Above $250,000 to $500,000	$2,000
Above $500,000 to $5,000,000	$3,000
Above $5,000,000	$4,000

When no amount can be stated at the time of filing, the filing fee is $1,000, subject to adjustment when the claim or counterclaim is disclosed.

When a claim or counterclaim is not for a monetary amount, an appropriate filing fee will be determined by the AAA.

Hearing Fees

For each day of hearing held before a single arbitrator, an administrative fee of $100 is payable by each party

For each day of hearing held before a multiarbitrator panel, an administrative fee of $150 is payable by each party.

Postponement Fees

A fee of $50 is payable by a party causing a postponement of any hearing scheduled before a single arbitrator.

A fee of $150 is payable by a party causing a postponement of any hearing scheduled before a multiarbitrator panel.

Processing Fees

No processing fee is payable until 180 days after a case is initiated.

On single-arbitrator cases, a processing fee of $150 per party is payable 180 days after the case is initiated, and every 90 days thereafter, until the case is withdrawn or settled or the hearings are closed by the arbitrator.

On multiarbitrator cases, a processing fee of $200 per party is payable 180 days after the case is initiated, and every 90 days thereafter, until the case is withdrawn or settled or the hearings are closed by the arbitrators.

Suspension for Nonpayment

If arbitrator compensation or administrative charges have not been paid in full, the AAA may so inform the parties in order that one of them may make the required payment. If such payments are not made, the arbitrator may order the suspension or termination of the proceedings. If no arbitrator has yet been appointed, the AAA may suspend the proceedings in such a situation.

Hearing Room Rental

Rooms for hearings are available on a rental basis. Check with our local office for availability and rates.

CODE OF ARBITRATION PROCEDURE

[Code adopted effective November 1, 1968]

PART I. ADMINISTRATIVE PROVISIONS

¶3701   Matters Eligible for Submission

Sec. 1. This Code of Arbitration Procedure is prescribed and adopted pursuant to Article VII, Section 1(a)(3) of the By-Laws of the National Association of Securities Dealers, Inc., (the Association) for the arbitration of any dispute, claim or controversy arising out of or in connection with the business of any member of the Association, with the exception of disputes involving the insurance business of any member which is also an insurance company:

(1) between or among members;

(2) between or among members and public customers, or others; and

(3) between or among members, registered clearing agencies with which the Association has entered into an agreement to utilize the Association's arbitration facilities and procedures, and participants, pledgees or other persons using the facilities of a registered clearing agency, as these terms are defined under the rules of such a registered clearing agency.

[Sec. 1 amended effective May 7, 1991.]

¶3702   National Arbitration Committee

Sec. 2. The Board of Governors of the Association, following the annual election of members to the Board, shall appoint a National Arbitration Committee of such size and composition, including representation from the public at large, as it shall deem appropriate and in the public interest. The Chairman of the Committee shall be named by the Chairman of the Board. The said Committee shall establish and maintain a pool of arbitrators composed of persons from within and without the securities industry.

The Committee shall have the authority to establish appropriate rules, regulations and procedures to govern the conduct of all arbitration matters before the Association. All rules, regulations and procedures and amendments there to promulgated by the Committee must be by a majority vote of all the members of the said Committee. It shall also have such other power and authority as is necessary to effectuate the purposes of this Code.

The Committee shall meet at least once each year and at such other times as are deemed necessary by the Committee.

¶3703   Director of Arbitration

Sec. 3. The Board of Governors of the Association shall appoint a Director of Arbitration who shall be charged with the performance of all administrative duties and functions in connection with matters submitted for arbitration pursuant to this Code. He shall be directly responsible to the National Arbitration Committee and shall report to it at periodic intervals established by the Committee and at such other times as called upon by the Committee to do so.

¶3704   Composition and Appointment of Panels
Sec. 4. The Director of Arbitration shall compose and appoint panels of arbitrators from the existing pool of arbitrators of the Association to conduct the arbitration of any matter which shall be eligible for submission under this Code. The Director of Arbitration may request that the Executive Committee of the National Arbitration Committee undertake the composition and appointment of a panel or undertake consultation with the Executive Committee regarding the composition and appointment of a panel in any circumstances where he determines such action to be appropriate.

- **Resolution of the Board of Governors**
  RESOLVED that all persons serving on panels of arbitrators pursuant to Section 4 of the Association's Code of Arbitration Procedure shall be paid an honorarium for each hearing session in which they participate while in the performance of said duties.
  The honorarium shall be $150 for a single session, $225 for a double session, $50 for travel to a cancelled hearing, and $50 per day additional honorarium to the chairperson of the panel. The honorarium for a case not requiring a hearing is $75 per case.
  (Resolution adopted effective June 14, 1977; amended May 30, 1980; amended February 8, 1982; amended January 14, 1987.)

¶3705   Non-Waiver of Association Objects and Purposes
Sec. 5. The submission of any matter to arbitration under this Code shall in no way limit or preclude any right, action or determination by the Association which it would otherwise be authorized to adopt, administer or enforce.

¶3706   Legal Proceedings
Sec. 6. No party shall, during the arbitration of any matter, prosecute or commence any suit, action or proceeding against any other party touching upon any of the matters referred to arbitration pursuant to this Code.

¶3707   Amendment, Modification or Cancellation of Code
Sec. 7. This Code may, upon a majority vote of the Board of Governors, be altered, amended, modified or canceled.

- **Selected NASD Notice to Members**
  Transitional period for implementation of SEC Rule 15c2-2 to cease as of January 1, 1985.
  (December 26, 1984)

PART II. INDUSTRY AND CLEARING CONTROVERSIES

¶3708   Required Submission
Sec. 8. (a) Any dispute, claim or controversy eligible for under Part I of this code between or among members and/or associated persons, and/or certain others, arising in connection with the business of such

member(s) or in connection with the activities of such associated person(s), shall be arbitrated under this Code, at the instance of:

(1) a member against another member;

(2) a member against a person associated with a member or a person associated with a member against a member; and,

(3) a person associated with a member against a person associated with a member.

(b) Any dispute, claim or controversy involving an act or failure to act by a clearing member, a registered clearing agency, or participants, pledgees or other persons using the facilities of a registered clearing agency, under the rules of any registered clearing agency with which the Association has entered into an agreement to utilize the Association's arbitration facilities and procedures shall be arbitrated in accordance with such agreement and the rules of such registered clearing agency.

¶3709   Composition of Panels

Sec. 9. (a) Except as otherwise provided in Section 10 of the Code, in all arbitration matters between or among members and/or persons associated with members, and where the amount in controversy does not exceed $30,000, the Director of Arbitration shall appoint a single arbitrator to decide the matter in controversy. The arbitrator chosen shall be from the securities industry. Upon the request of a party in its initial filing or the arbitrator, the Director of Arbitration shall appoint a panel of three (3) arbitrators, all of whom shall be from the securities industry.

(b) In all arbitration matters between or among members and/or persons associated with members and where the amount in controversy exceeds $30,000, a panel shall consist of three arbitrators, all of whom shall be from the securities industry.

[Amended effective May 10, 1989.]

¶3710   Simplified Industry Arbitration

Sec. 10. (a) Any dispute, claim or controversy arising between or among members or associated persons submitted to arbitration under this Code involving a dollar amount not exceeding $10,000, exclusive of attendant costs shall be resolved by an arbitration panel constituted pursuant to the provisions of subsection (1) hereof solely upon the pleadings and documentary evidence filed by the parties, unless one of the parties to the proceeding files with the Office of the Director of Arbitration within ten (10) business days following the filing of the last pleading a request for a hearing of the matter.

(1) In any proceeding pursuant to this section, an arbitration panel shall consist of no fewer than one (1) but no more than three (3) arbitrators, all of whom shall be from within the securities industry.

(2) Notwithstanding the provisions of this section, any member of an arbitration panel constituted pursuant to this section shall be authorized to request the submission of further documentary evidence in a proceeding and any such panel may by majority vote call and conduct a hearing if such is deemed to be necessary.

(b) All awards rendered in proceedings pursuant to subsection (a) hereof shall be made within thirty (30) business days from the date the

arbitrators review all of the written statements, documents and other evidentiary material filed by the parties and declare the matter closed.
[Amended effective May 10,1989.]

¶3711   Applicability of Uniform Code
Sec. 11. Except as otherwise provided in this Part, the rules and procedures applicable to arbitrations concerning industry and clearing controversies shall be those set forth hereinafter under Part III.

PART III. UNIFORM CODE OF ARBITRATION

¶3712   Required Submission
Sec. 12. (a) Any dispute, claim or controversy eligible for submission under Part I of this Code between a customer and a member and/or associated person arising in connection with the business of such member or in connection with the activities of such associated persons shall be arbitrated under this Code, as provided by any duly executed and enforceable written agreement or upon the demand of the customer.

(b) Under this Code, the Director of Arbitration, upon approval of the Executive Committee of the National Arbitration Committee or the National Arbitration Committee, shall have the right to decline the use of its arbitration facilities in any dispute, claim or controversy, where, having due regard for the purposes of the Association and intent of this Code such dispute, claim or controversy is not a proper subject matter arbitration.

(c) Claims which arise out of transactions in a readily identifiable market may, by the consent of the Claimant, be referred to the arbitration forum for that market by the Association.

(d) Class Action Claims.

(1) A claim submitted as a class action shall not be eligible for arbitration under this Code at the Association.

(2) Any claim filed by a member or members of a putative or certified class action is also ineligible for arbitration at the Association if the claim is encompassed by a putative or certified class action filed in federal or state court, or is ordered by a court to an arbitral forum not sponsored by a self-regulatory organization for classwide arbitration. However, such claims shall be eligible for arbitration in accordance with Section 12(a) or pursuant to the parties' contractual agreement, if any, if a claimant demonstrates that it has elected not to participate in the putative or certified class action or, if applicable, has complied with any conditions for withdrawing from the class prescribed by the court.

Disputes concerning whether a particular claim is encompassed by a putative or certified class action shall be referred by the Director of Arbitration to a panel of arbitrators in accordance with Section 13 or Section 19 of the Code, as applicable. Either party may elect instead to petition the court with jurisdiction over the putative or certified class action to resolve such disputes. Any such petition to the court must be filed within ten business days of receipt of notice that the Director of Arbitration is referring the dispute to a panel of arbitrators.

(3) No member or associated person shall seek to enforce any agreement to arbitrate against a customer who has initiated in court a putative

class action or is a member of a putative or certified class with respect to any claims encompassed by the class action unless and until: (A) the class certification is denied; (B) the class is decertified; (C) the customer is excluded from the class by the court; or (D) the customer elects not to participate in the putative or certified class action or, if applicable, has complied with any conditions for withdrawing from the class prescribed by the court.

(4) No member or associated person shall be deemed to have waived any of its rights under this Code or under any agreement to arbitrate to which it is party except to the extent stated in this paragraph.

[Amended effective January 8, 1992; October 28, 1992.]

- **Selected NASD Notices to Members**

84–51 Approval by the SEC of amendment to the Association's Code of Arbitration Procedures to conform to recent amendments of the Uniform Arbitration Code.

(September 28, 1984)

92–65 SEC Approval of Amendments Concerning Exclusion of Class-Action Matters from Arbitration Proceedings and Requiring That Predispute Arbitration Agreements Include a Notice that Class-Action Matters May Not be Arbitrated

(December 1992)

¶3713   Simplified Arbitration

Sec. 13. (a) Any dispute, claim or controversy, arising between a public customer(s) and an associated person or a member subject to arbitration under this Code involving a dollar amount not exceeding $10,000.00, exclusive of attendant costs and interest, shall be arbitrated as hereinafter provided.

(b) The Claimant shall file with the Director of Arbitration an executed Submission Agreement and a copy of the Statement of Claim of the controversy in dispute and the required deposit, together with documents in support of the Claim. Sufficient additional copies of the Submission Agreement and the Statement of Claim and supporting documents shall be provided to the Director of Arbitration for each party and the arbitrator. The Statement of Claim shall specify the relevant facts the remedies sought and whether or not a hearing is demanded.

(c) The Claimant shall pay a non-refundable filing fee and shall remit a hearing session deposit as specified in Section 43 of this Code upon filing of the Submission Agreement. The final disposition of the fee or deposit shall be determined by the arbitrator.

(d) The Director of Arbitration shall endeavor to serve promptly by mail or otherwise on the Respondent(s) one (1) copy of the Submission Agreement and one (1) copy of the Statement of Claim. Within twenty (20) calendar days from receipt of the Statement of Claim, Respondent(s) shall serve each party with an executed Submission Agreement and a copy of Respondent's Answer. Respondent's executed Submission Agreement and Answer shall also be filed with the Director of Arbitration with sufficient additional copies for the arbitrator(s) along with any deposit required under the schedule of fees for customer disputes. The Answer shall designate all available defenses to the Claim and may set forth any related Counterclaim and/or related Third-Party Claim the Respondent(s) may have against the Claimant or any other person. If the Respondent(s) has interposed a Third-Party Claim, the Respondent(s) shall serve the Third-Party Respondent with an executed Submission Agreement, a copy of Respondent's Answer containing the Third-Party Claim, and a copy of the original Claim filed by the Claimant. The Third-Party Respondent shall respond in the manner herein provided for response to the Claim. If the Respondent(s) files a related Counterclaim exceeding $10,000, the arbitrator may refer the Claim, Counterclaim and/or Third-Party Claim, if any, to a panel of three (3) or five (5) arbitrators in accordance with Section 19 of this Code or, he may dismiss the Counterclaim and/or Third-Party Claim without prejudice to the Counterclaimant(s) and/or Third-Party Claimant(s) pursuing the Counterclaim and/or Third-Party Claim in a separate proceeding. The costs to the Claimant under either proceeding shall in no event exceed the total amount specified in Section 43.

(e) All parties shall serve on all other parties and the Director of Arbitration, with sufficient additional copies for the arbitrator(s), a copy of the Answer, Counterclaim, Third Party Claim, Amended Claim, or other responsive pleading, if any. The Claimant, if a Counterclaim is asserted against him, shall within ten (10) calendar days either (i) serve on each party and on the Director of Arbitration, with sufficient additional copies for the arbitrator(s), a Reply to any Counterclaim or, (ii) if the amount of the Counterclaim exceeds the Claim, shall have the right to file a statement withdrawing the Claim. If the Claimant withdraws the Claim, the proceedings shall be discontinued without prejudice to the rights of the parties.

(f) The dispute, claim or controversy shall be submitted to a single public arbitrator knowledgeable in the securities industry selected by the Director of Arbitration. Unless the public customer demands or consents to a hearing, or the arbitrator calls a hearing, the arbitrator shall decide the dispute, claim or controversy solely upon the pleadings and evidence filed by the parties. If a hearing is necessary, such hearing shall be held as soon as practicable at a locale selected by the Director of Arbitration.

(g) The Director of Arbitration may grant extensions of time to file any pleading upon a showing of good cause.

(h) (i) The arbitrator shall be authorized to require the submission of further documentary evidence as he, in his sole discretion, deems advisable:

(ii) If a hearing is demanded or consented to in accordance with Section 13(f), the General Provisions Governing Pre-Hearing Proceedings under Section 32 shall apply.

(iii) If no hearing is demanded or consented to, all requests for document production shall be submitted in writing to the Director of Arbitration within ten (10) business days of notification of the identity of the arbitrator selected to decide the case. The requesting party shall serve simultaneously its requests for document production on all parties. Any response or objections to the requested document production shall be served on all parties and filed with the Director of Arbitration within five (5) business days of receipt of the requests for production. The selected arbitrator shall resolve all requests under this section on the papers submitted.

(i) Upon the request of the arbitrator, the Director of Arbitration shall appoint two (2) additional arbitrators to the panel which shall decide the matter in controversy.

(j) In any case where there is more than one (1) arbitrator, the majority shall be public arbitrators.

(k) In his discretion, the arbitrator may, at the request of any party, permit such party to submit additional documentation relating to the pleadings.

(l) Except as otherwise provided herein, the general arbitration rules of the association shall be applicable to proceedings instituted under this Section.

[Amended effective October 1, 1984; April 1, 1988; May 10, 1989; June 1, 1990; April 26, 1991; January 8, 1992; September 8, 1992.]

• Interpretation of the Board of Governors

Related Counterclaim

As used in this Section 13, the term "related Counterclaim" shall mean any Counterclaim related to a customer's accounts with a member.

¶3714 Hearing Requirements-Waiver of Hearing

Sec. 14. (a) Any dispute, claim or controversy except as provided in Section 10 Simplified Industry Arbitration) or Section 13 (Simplified Arbitration), shall require a hearing unless all parties waive such hearing in writing and request that the matter be resolved solely upon the pleadings and documentary evidence.

(b) Notwithstanding a written waiver of a hearing by the parties, a majority of the arbitrators may call for and conduct a hearing. In addition, any arbitrator may request he submission of further evidence.

¶3715 Time Limitation Upon Submission

Sec. 15. No dispute, claim, or controversy shall be eligible for submission to arbitration under this Code where six (6) years have elapsed from the occurrence or event giving rise to the act or dispute, claim or controversy. This section shall not extend applicable statutes of limitations, nor shall it apply to any case which is directed to arbitration by a court of competent jurisdiction.

[Amended effective October 1, 1984.]

¶3716 Dismissal of Proceedings

Sec. 16. At any time during the course of an arbitration, the arbitrators may, either upon their own initiative or at the request of a party, dismiss the proceeding and refer the parties to the remedies provided by applicable law. The arbitrators shall at the joint request of all the parties dismiss the proceedings.

¶3717 Settlements

Sec. 17. All settlements upon any matter shall be at the election of the parties.

¶3718   Tolling of Time Limitation(s) for the Institution of Legal Proceedings and Extension of Time Limitation(s) for Submission to Arbitration

Sec. 18. (a) Where permitted by applicable law, the time limitations which would otherwise run or accrue for the institution of legal proceedings shall be tolled where a duly executed Submission Agreement is filed by the Claimant(s). The tolling shall continue for such period as the Association shall retain jurisdiction upon the matter submitted.

(b) The six (6) year time limitation upon submission to arbitration shall not apply when the parties have submitted the dispute, claim or controversy to a court of competent jurisdiction. The six (6) year time limitation shall not run for such period as the court shall retain jurisdiction upon the matter submitted.

[Amended effective October 1, 1984.]

¶3719   Designation of Number of Arbitrators

Sec. 19. (a) Except as otherwise provided in Section 13 in this Code, in all arbitration matters involving public customers and where the amount in controversy does not exceed $30,000, the Director of Arbitration shall appoint a single public arbitrator knowledgeable in but who is not from the securities industry to decide the dispute, claim or controversy. Upon the request of a party in its initial filing or the arbitrator, the Director of Arbitration shall appoint a panel of three (3) arbitrators which shall decide the matter in controversy. At least a majority of the arbitrators appointed shall not be from the securities industry, unless the public customer requests a panel consisting of at least a majority from the securities industry.

(b) In arbitration matters involving public customers and where the amount in controversy exceeds $30,000, or where the matter in controversy does not involve or disclose a money claim, the Director of Arbitration shall appoint an arbitration panel which consists of no fewer than three (3) nor more than five (5) arbitrators, at least a majority of whom shall not be from the securities industry, unless the public customer requests a panel consisting of at least a majority from the securities industry.

(c) An arbitrator will be deemed as being from the securities industry if he or she:

(1) is a person associated with a member or other broker/dealer, municipal securities dealer, government securities broker, or government securities dealer, or

(2) has been associated with any of the above within the past three (3) years, or

(3) is retired from any of the above, or

(4) is an attorney, accountant, or other professional who has devoted twenty (20) percent or more of his or her professional work effort to securities industry clients within the last two years, or

(5) is an individual who is registered under the Commodity Exchange Act or is a member of a registered futures association or any commodities exchange or is associated with any such person(s).

(d) An arbitrator who is not from the securities industry shall be deemed a public arbitrator. A person will not be classified as a public arbitrator if he or she has a spouse or other member of the household who is a person who is associated with a member or other broker/dealer, municipal securities dealer, government securities broker, or government securities dealer.

[Amended effective July 1, 1986; April 1, 1988; May 10, 1989; October 7, 1992.]

¶3720 Composition of Panels
Sec. 20. The individuals who shall serve on a particular arbitration panel shall be determined by the Director of Arbitration. The Director of Arbitration may name the chairman of the panel.

¶3721 Notice of Selection of Arbitrators
Sec. 21. The Director of Arbitration shall inform the parties of the arbitrators names and employment histories for the past ten (10) years, as well as information disclosed pursuant to Section 23, at least eight (8) business days prior to the date fixed for the first hearing session. A party may make further inquiry of the Director of Arbitration concerning an arbitrator's background. In the event that prior to the first hearing session, any arbitrator should become disqualified, resign, die, refuse or otherwise be unable to perform as an arbitrator, the Director of Arbitration shall appoint a replacement arbitrator to fill the vacancy on the panel. The Director of Arbitration shall inform the parties as soon as possible of the name and employment history of the replacement arbitrator for the past ten years, as well as information disclosed pursuant to Section 23. A party may make further inquiry of the Director of Arbitration concerning the replacement arbitrator's background and within the time remaining prior to the first hearing session or the five (5) day period provided under Section 22, whichever is shorter, may exercise its right to challenge the replacement arbitrator as provided in Section 22.

[Amended effective September 19, 1988; May 10, 1989.]

¶3722 Peremptory Challenge
Sec. 22. In any arbitration proceeding, each party shall have the right to one peremptory challenge. In arbitrations where there are multiple Claimants, Respondents and/or Third-Party Respondents, the Claimants shall have one peremptory challenge, the Respondents shall have one peremptory challenge and the Third-Party Respondents shall have one peremptory challenge, unless the Director of Arbitration determines that the interests of justice would best be served by awarding additional peremptory challenges. Unless extended by the Director of Arbitration, a party wishing to exercise a peremptory challenge must do so by notifying the Director of Arbitration in writing within five (5) business days of notification of the identity of the person(s) named under Section 21 or Section 32(d) or (e), whichever comes first. There shall be unlimited challenges for cause.

[Amended effective October 1,1984; January 8, 1992.]

¶3723 Disclosures Required of Arbitrators

Sec. 23. (a) Each arbitrator shall be required to disclose to the Director of Arbitration any circumstances which might preclude such arbitrator from rendering an objective and impartial determination. Each arbitrator shall disclose:

(1) Any direct or indirect financial or personal interest in the outcome of the arbitration;

(2) Any existing or past financial, business, professional, family, or social relationships that are likely to affect impartiality or might reasonably create an appearance of partiality or bias. Persons requested to serve as arbitrators should disclose any such relationships that they personally have with any party or its counsel, or with any individual whom they have been told will be a witness. They should also disclose any such relationship involving members of their families or their current employers, partners, or business associates.

(b) Persons who are requested to accept appointment as arbitrators should make a reasonable effort to inform themselves of any interests or relationships described in Paragraph (a) above.

(c) The obligation to disclose interests, relationships, or circumstances that might preclude an arbitrator from rendering an objective and impartial determination described in subsection (a) hereof is a continuing duty that requires a person who accepts appointment as an arbitrator to disclose, at any stage of the arbitration, any such interests, relationships, or circumstances that arise, or are recalled or discovered.

(d) Prior to the commencement of the first hearing session, the Director of Arbitration may remove an arbitrator based on information disclosed pursuant to this section. The Director of Arbitration shall also inform the parties of any information disclosed pursuant to this Section if the arbitrator who disclosed the information is not removed.

[Amended effective May 10,1989.]

¶3724   Disqualification or Other Disability of Arbitrators

Sec. 24. In the event that any arbitrator, after the commencement of the first hearing session but prior to the rendition of the award, should become disqualified, resign, die, refuse or otherwise be unable to perform as an arbitrator, the remaining arbitrator(s) shall continue with the hearing and determination of the controversy, unless such continuation is objected to by any party within five (5) days of notification of the vacancy on the panel. Upon objection, the Director of Arbitration shall appoint a replacement arbitrator to fill the vacancy and the hearing shall continue. The Director of Arbitration shall inform the parties as soon as possible of the name and employment history of the replacement arbitrator for the past ten years, as well as information disclosed pursuant to Section 23. A party may make further inquiry of the Director of Arbitration concerning the replacement arbitrator's background and within the time remaining prior to the next scheduled hearing session or the five (5) day period provided under Section 22, whichever is shorter, may exercise its right to challenge the replacement arbitrator as provided in Section 22.

[Amended effective September 19, 1988.]

¶3725   Initiation of Proceedings

Sec. 25. Except as otherwise provided herein, an arbitration proceeding under this Code shall be instituted as follows:

Statement of Claim

(a) The Claimant shall file with the Director of Arbitration an executed Submission Agreement, a Statement of Claim of the controversy in dispute, together with the documents in support of the Claim and the required deposit. Sufficient additional copies of the Submission Agreement and the Statement of Claim and supporting documents shall be provided to the Director of Arbitration for each party and each arbitrator. The Statement of Claim shall specify the relevant facts and the remedies sought. The Director of Arbitration shall endeavor to serve promptly by mail or otherwise on the Respondent(s) one (1) copy of the Submission Agreement and one (1) copy of the Statement of Claim.

Answer-Defenses, Counterclaims and/or Cross-Claims

(b)(1) Within twenty (20) business days from receipt of the Statement of Claim, Respondent(s) shall serve each party with an executed Submission Agreement and a copy of Respondent's Answer. Respondent's executed Submission Agreement and Answer shall also be filed with the Director of Arbitration with sufficient additional copies for the arbitrator(s) along with any deposit required under the schedule of fees. The Answer shall specify all available defenses and relevant facts thereto that will be relied upon at hearing and may set forth any related Counterclaim the Respondent(s) may have against the Claimant, any Cross-Claim the Respondent(s) may have against any other named Respondent(s), and any Third-Party Claim against any other party or person based upon any existing dispute, claim or controversy subject to arbitration under this Code

(2)(i) A Respondent, Responding Claimant, Cross-Claimant, Cross-Respondent, or Third-Party Respondent who pleads only a general denial as an answer may, upon objection by a party, in the discretion of the arbitrators, be barred from presenting any facts or defenses at the time of the hearing.

(ii) A Respondent, Responding Claimant, Cross-Claimant, Cross-Respondent, or Third-Party Respondent who fails to specify all available defenses and relevant facts in such party's answer may, upon objection by a party, in the discretion of the arbitrators, be barred from presenting such facts or defenses not included in such party's answer at the hearing.

(iii) A Respondent, Responding Claimant, Cross-Claimant, Cross-Respondent, or Third-Party Respondent who fails to file an answer within twenty (20) business days from receipt of service of a claim, unless the time to answer has been extended pursuant to paragraph (5), below, may, in the discretion of the arbitrators, be barred from presenting any matter, arguments or defenses at the hearing.

(3) Respondent(s) shall serve each party with a copy of any Third-Party Claim. The Third Party Claim shall also be filed with the Director of Arbitration with sufficient additional copies for the arbitrator(s) along with any deposit required under the schedule of fees. Third-Party Respon-

dent(s) shall answer in the manner provided for response to the Claim, as provided in paragraphs (1) and (2) above.

(4) The Claimant shall serve each party with a Reply to a Counterclaim within ten (10) days of receipt of an Answer containing a Counterclaim. The Reply shall also be filed with the Director of Arbitration with sufficient additional copies for the arbitrator(s).

(5) The time period to file any pleading, whether such be denominated as a Claim, Answer, Counterclaim, Cross-claim, Reply, or Third-Party pleading, may be extended for such further period as may be granted by the Director of Arbitration.

Service and Filing With the Director of Arbitration

(c)(1) Service may be effected by mail or other means of delivery. Service and filing are accomplished on the date of mailing either by first-class postage pre-paid or by means of overnight mail service or, in the case of other means of service, on the date of delivery. Filing with the Director of Arbitration shall be made on the same date as service on a party.

(2) If a member firm and a person associated with the member firm are named parties to an arbitration proceeding at the time of the filing of the Statement of Claim, service on the person associated with the member firm may be made on the associated person or the member firm, which shall perfect service upon the associated person. If the member firm does not undertake to represent the associated person, the member firm shall serve the associated person with the Statement of Claim, shall advise all parties and the Director of Arbitration of that fact, and shall provide such associated person's current address.

Joinder and Consolidation-Multiple Parties

(d)(1) Permissive Joinder. All persons may join in one action as claimants if they assert any right to relief jointly, severally, or arising out of the same transaction, occurrence or series of transactions or occurrences and if any questions of law or fact common to all these claimants will arise in the action. All persons may be joined in one action as respondents if there is asserted against them jointly or severally, any right to relief arising out of the same transaction, occurrence or series of transactions or occurrences and if any questions of law or fact common to all respondents will arise in the action. A claimant or respondent need not assert rights to or defend against all the relief demanded. Judgment may be given for one or more of the claimants according to their respective rights to relief, and against one or more respondents according to the irrespective liabilities.

(2) In arbitrations where there are multiple Claimants, Respondents and/or Third Party Respondents, the Director of Arbitration shall be authorized to determine preliminarily whether such parties should proceed in the same or separate arbitrations. Such determination will be considered subsequent to the filing of all responsive pleadings.

(3) The Director of Arbitration shall be authorized to determine preliminarily whether claims filed separately are related and shall be authorized to consolidate such claims for hearing and award purposes.

(4) Further determinations with respect to joinder, consolidation, and multiple parties under this subsection shall be made by the arbitration panel and shall be deemed final.

[Amended effective October 1, 1984; July 1, 1986; May 10, 1989; May 7, 1991.]

¶3726 Designation of Time and Place of Hearings
Sec. 26. The time and place of the initial hearing shall be determined by the Director of Arbitration and each hearing thereafter by the arbitrators. Notice of the time and place for the initial hearing shall be given at least eight (8) business days prior to the date fixed for the hearing by personal service, registered or certified mail to each of the parties unless the parties shall, by their mutual consent, waive the notice provisions under this Section. Notice for each hearing thereafter shall be given as the arbitrators may determine. Attendance at a hearing waives notice thereof.

[Amended effective May 7, 1991.]

¶3727 Representation by Counsel
Sec. 27. All parties shall have the right to representation by counsel at any stage of the proceedings.

¶3728 Attendance at Hearings
Sec. 28. The attendance or presence of all persons at hearings including witnesses shall be determined by the arbitrators. However, all parties to the arbitration and their counsel shall be entitled to attend all hearings.

- **Policy of the Board of Governors**
In response to recent questions concerning the order of closing argument in arbitration proceedings conducted under the auspices of the National Association of Securities Dealers, Inc., it is the practice in these proceedings to allow claimants to proceed first in closing argument, with rebuttal argument being permitted. Claimants may reserve their entire closing for rebuttal. The hearing procedures may, however, be varied in the discretion of the arbitrators, provided all parties are allowed a full and fair opportunity to present their respective cases.

¶3729 Failure to Appear
Sec. 29. If any of the parties, after due notice, fails to appear at a hearing or at any continuation of a hearing session, the arbitrators may, in their discretion, proceed with the arbitration of the controversy. In such cases, all awards shall be rendered as if each party had entered an appearance in the matter submitted.

[Amended effective January 8, 1992.]

¶3730 Adjournments
Sec. 30. (a) The arbitrator(s) may, in their discretion, adjourn any hearing(s) whether upon their own initiative or upon the request of any party to the arbitration.

(b) Unless waived by the Director of Arbitration upon a showing of financial need, party requesting an adjournment after arbitrators have been appointed shall deposit with the request for an adjournment, a fee equal to the initial deposit of hearing session fees for the first adjournment and twice the initial deposit of hearing session fees, not to exceed $1,000, for a second or subsequent adjournment requested by that party. If the adjournment is not granted, the deposit shall he refunded. If the adjournment is not granted, the arbitrator(s) may direct the return of the adjournment fee.

(c) Upon receiving a third request consented to by all parties for an adjournment, the arbitrator(s) may dismiss the arbitration without prejudice to the Claimant filing a arbitration.

[Amended effective July 1, 1986; June 1, 1990; December 30, 1991.]

¶3731   Acknowledgement of Pleadings
Sec. 31. The arbitrators shall acknowledge to all parties present that they have read the pleadings filed by the parties.

¶3732   General Provisions Governing Pre-Hearing Proceedings
Sec. 32. (a) Requests for Documents and Information. The parties shall cooperate to the fullest extent practicable in the voluntary exchange of documents and information to expedite the arbitration. Any request for documents or other information should be specific, relate to the matter in controversy, and afford the party to whom the request is made a reasonable period of time to respond without interfering with time set for the hearing.

(b) Document Production and Information Exchange.

(1) Any party may serve a written request for information or documents ("information request") upon another party twenty (20) business days or more after service of the Statement of Claim by the Director of Arbitration or upon filing of the Answer, whichever is earlier. The requesting party shall serve the information request on all parties and file a copy with the Director of Arbitration. The parties shall endeavor to resolve disputes regarding an information request prior to serving any objection to the request. Such efforts shall be set forth in the objection.

(2) Unless a greater time is allowed by the requesting party, information requests shall be satisfied or objected to within thirty (30) calendar days from the date of service. Any objection to an information request shall be served by the objecting party on all parties and filed with the Director of Arbitration.

(3) Any response to objections to an information request shall be served on all parties and filed with the Director of Arbitration within ten (10) calendar days of receipt of the objection.

(4) Upon the written request of a party whose information request is unsatisfied, the matter will be referred by the Director of Arbitration to either a pre-hearing conference under subsection (d) of this section or to a selected arbitrator under subsection (e) of this section.

(c) Pre-Hearing Exchange. At least ten (10) calendar days prior to the first scheduled hearing date, all parties shall serve on each other copies of documents in their possession they intend to present at the hearing and shall identify witnesses they intend to present at the hearing. The arbitrators may exclude from the arbitration any documents not exchanged or witnesses not identified. This paragraph does not require service of copies of documents or identification of witnesses which parties may use for cross-examination or rebuttal.

(d) Pre-Hearing Conference

(1) Upon the written request of a party, an arbitrator, or at the discretion of the Director of Arbitration, a pre-hearing conference shall be scheduled. The Director of Arbitration shall set the time and place of a pre-hearing conference and appoint a person to preside. The pre-hearing conference may be held by telephone conference call. The presiding person shall seek to achieve agreement among the parties on any issue which relates to the pre-hearing process or to the hearing, including but not limited to exchange of information, exchange or production of documents, identification of witnesses, identification and exchange of hearing documents, stipulation of facts, identification and briefing of contested issues, and any other matters which will expedite the arbitration proceedings.

(2) Any issues raised at the pre-hearing conference that are not resolved maybe referred to a single member of the arbitration panel for decision.

(e) Decisions by Selected Arbitrator. The Director of Arbitration may appoint a single member of the arbitration panel to decide all unresolved issues under this section. In matters involving public customers, such single arbitrator shall be a public arbitrator, except that the arbitrator may be either public or industry when the public customer has requested a panel consisting of a majority from the securities industry. Such arbitrator shall be authorized to act on behalf of the panel to issue subpoenas, direct appearances of witnesses and production of documents, set deadlines for compliance, and issue any other ruling which will expedite the arbitration proceedings. Decisions under this section shall be made upon the papers submitted by the parties, unless the arbitrator calls a hearing. The arbitrator may elect to refer any issue under this section to the full panel.

[Amended effective May 10, 1989.]

¶3733   Subpoenas and Power to Direct Appearances

Sec. 33. (a) Subpoenas. The arbitrators and any counsel of record to the proceeding shall have the power of the subpoena process as provided by law. All parties shall be given a copy of a subpoena upon its issuance. Parties shall produce witnesses and present proofs to the fullest extent possible without resort to the subpoena process.

(b) Power to Direct Appearances and Production of Documents. The arbitrator(s)shall be empowered without resort to the subpoena process to direct the appearance of any person employed or associated with any member of the Association and/or the production of any records in the possession or control of such persons or members. Unless the arbitrator(s) direct otherwise, the party requesting the appearance of a person or the production of documents under this Section shall bear all reasonable costs of such appearance and/or production.

[Amended effective May 10, 1989.]

¶3734   Evidence

Sec. 34. The arbitrators shall determine the materiality and relevance of any evidence proffered and shall not be bound by rules governing the admissibility of evidence.

¶3735 Interpretation of Provisions of Code and Enforcement of Arbitrator Rulings

Sec. 35. The arbitrators shall be empowered to interpret and determine the applicability of all provisions under this Code and to take appropriate action to obtain compliance with any ruling by the arbitrator(s). Such interpretations and actions to obtain compliance shall be final and binding upon the parties.

[Amended effective November 16, 1992.]

¶3736 Determination of Arbitrators

Sec. 36. All rulings and determinations of the panel shall be by a majority of the arbitrators.

¶3737 Record of Proceedings

Sec. 37. A verbatim record by stenographic reporter or tape recording of all arbitration hearings shall be kept. If a party or parties to a dispute elect to have the record transcribed, the cost of such transcription shall be borne by the party or parties making the request unless the arbitrators direct otherwise. The arbitrators may also direct that the record be transcribed. If the record is transcribed at the request of any party, a copy shall be provided to the arbitrators.

[Amended effective May 10, 1989.]

¶3738 Oaths of the Arbitrators and Witnesses

Sec. 38. Prior to the commencement of the first session, an oath or affirmation shall be administered to the arbitrators. All testimony shall be under oath or affirmation.

¶3739 Amendments

Sec. 39. (a) After the filing of any pleadings, if a party desires to file a new or different pleading, such change must be made in writing and filed with the Director of Arbitration with sufficient additional copies for each arbitrator. The party filing a new or different pleading shall serve on all other parties, a copy of the new or different pleading in accordance with the provisions set forth in Section 25(b). The other parties may, within ten (10) business days from the receipt of service, file a response with all other parties and the Director of Arbitration in accordance with Section 25(b).

(b) After a panel has been appointed, 110 new or different pleading may be filed except for a responsive pleading as provided for in (a) above or with the panel's consent.

[Amended effective October 1, 1984; April 26, 1991.]

¶3740 Reopening of Hearings

Sec. 40. Where permitted by applicable law, the hearings may be reopened by the arbitrators on their own motion or in the discretion of the arbitrators upon application of a party at any time before the award is rendered.

¶3741 Awards

Sec. 41. (a) All awards shall be in writing and signed by a majority of the arbitrators or in such manner as is required by applicable law. Such awards may be entered as a judgment in any court of competent jurisdiction.

(b) Unless the applicable law directs otherwise, all awards rendered pursuant to this Code shall be deemed final and not subject to review or appeal.

(c) The Director of Arbitration shall endeavor to serve a copy of the award: (i) by registered or certified mail upon all parties, or their counsel, at the address of record; or, (ii) by personally serving the award upon the parties; or, (iii) by filing or delivering the award in such manner as may be authorized by law.

(d) The arbitrator(s) shall endeavor to render an award within thirty (30) business days from the date the record is closed.

(e) The award shall contain the names of the party the name of counsel, if any, a summary of the issues, including the type(s) of any security or product in controversy, the damages and other relief requested, the damages and other relief a statement of any other issues resolved, the names of the arbitrators, the dates the claim was filed and the award rendered, the number and dates of hearing sessions, the location of the hearings, and the signatures of the arbitrators concurring in the award.

(f) All awards involving public customers and their contents, excluding the names of the arbitrators, shall be made publicly available. A party to an arbitration involving a public customer may request that the Director of Arbitration provide copies of all awards rendered by the arbitrator(s) chosen to decide its case. A party wishing to obtain such information must notify the Director of Arbitration within three (3) business days of receipt of notification of the identity of the person(s) named to the panel.

(g) Fees and assessments imposed by the arbitrators under Sections 43 and 44 shall be paid immediately upon the receipt of the award by the parties. Payment of such fees shall not be deemed ratification of the award by the parties.

(h) All monetary awards shall be paid within thirty (30) days of receipt unless a motion to vacate has been filed with a court of competent jurisdiction. An award shall bear interest from the date of award: (i) if not paid within thirty (30) days of receipt, (ii) if the award is the subject of a motion to vacate which is denied, or (iii) as specified by the arbitrator(s) in the award. Interest shall be assessed at the legal rate, if any, then prevailing in the state where the award was rendered, or at a rate set by the arbitrator(s).

[Amended effective May 10, 1989; April 26, 1991; May 7, 1991; January 8, 1992.]

¶3742   Incorporation By Reference

Sec. 42. This Code shall be deemed a part of and incorporated by reference in every agreement to arbitrate under the rules of the National Association of Securities Dealers, Inc. including a duly executed Submission Agreement.

[Amended effective May 7,1991.]

¶3743   Schedule of Fees for Customer Disputes

257

Sec. 43. (a) At the time of filing a Claim, Counterclaim, Third Party Claim or Cross-Claim, a party shall pay a non-refundable filing fee and shall remit a hearing session deposit to the Association in the amounts indicated in the schedules below unless such fee or deposit is specifically waived by the Director of Arbitration.

Where multiple hearing sessions are required, the arbitrators may require any of the parties to make additional hearing deposits for each additional hearing session. In no event shall the amount deposited by all parties per hearing session exceed the amount of the largest initial hearing deposit made by any party under the schedules below.

(b) A hearing session is any meeting between the parties and the arbitrator(s), including a pre-hearing conference with an arbitrator, which lasts four (4) hours or less. The forum fee for a pre-hearing conference with an arbitrator shall be the amount set forth in the schedules below as a hearing session deposit for a hearing with a single arbitrator.

(c) The arbitrators, in their awards shall determine the amount chargeable to the parties as forum fees and shall determine who shall pay such forum fees. Forum fees agreable to the parties shall he assessed on a per hearing session basis, and the aggregate for each hearing session may equal but shall not exceed the amount of the largest initial hearing deposit deposited by any party, except in a case where claims have been joined subsequent to filing in which case hearing session fees shall he computed as provided in paragraph (d). The arbitrator(s) may determine in the award at a party shall reimburse to another party any non-refundable filing fee it has paid. If a customer is assessed forum fees in connection with an industry claim, forum fees assessed against the customer shall be based on the hearing deposit required under the industry claims schedule for the amount awarded to industry parties to be paid by the customer and not based on the size of the industry claim. No fees shall be assessed against a customer in connection with an industry claim that is dismissed; however, in cases where there is also a customer claim, the customer may be assessed forum fees based on the customer claim under the procedure set out above. Amounts deposited by party shall be applied against forum fees, if any. In addition to forum fees, the arbitrator(s) may determine in the award the amount of costs incurred pursuant to actions 30, 32, 33, and 37 and, unless applicable law directs otherwise, other costs and expenses of the parties and arbitrator(s) which are within the scope of the agreement of the parties. The arbitrator(s) shall determine by whom such costs shall be borne. If the hearing session fees are not assessed against a party who had made a hearing deposit, the hearing deposit will be refunded unless the arbitrators determine otherwise.

(d) For claims filed separately which are subsequently joined or consolidated under action 25(d) of this Code, the hearing deposit and forum fees assessable per hearing session after joinder or consolidation shall be based on the cumulative amount in dispute. The arbitrator(s) shall determine by whom such fees shall be borne.

(e) If the dispute, claim, or controversy does not involve, disclose, or specify a money claim, the non-refundable filing fee shall be $250 and the hearing session deposit be remitted by a party shall be $600 or such

258

greater or lesser amount as the Director Arbitration or the panel of arbitrators may require, but shall not exceed $1,000.

(f) The Association shall retain the total initial amount deposited as hearing session deposits by all the parties in any matter submitted and settled or withdrawn within eight business days of the first scheduled hearing session other than a prehearing conference.

(g) Any matter submitted and thereafter settled or withdrawn subsequent to the commencement of the first hearing session, including a pre-hearing conference with an arbitrator, shall be subject to an assessment of forum fees and costs incurred pursuant Sections 30, 32, 33, and 37 based on hearing sessions held and scheduled within eight business days after the Association receives notice that the matter has been settled or withdrawn. The arbitrator(s) shall determine by whom such forum fees and costs shall borne.

Schedule of Fees

For purposes of the schedule of fees, the term "claim" includes Claims, Counter Claims, Third Party Claims, and Cross-Claims. Any such claim made by a customer is a customer claim. Any such claim made by a member or associated person of a member is an industry claim.

Customer Claimant

Amount in Dispute (Exclusive of Interest and Expenses)	Claim Filing Fee	Hearing Session Deposit		
		Simplified[1]	One Arbitrator[2]	Three + Arbitrator[3]
$0.01–$1,000	$15	$15	$15	NA
$1000.01–$2,500	$25	$25	$25	NA
$2,500.01–$5,000	$50	$75	$100	NA
$5,000.01–$10,000	$75	$75	$200	NA
$10,000.01–$30,000	$100	NA	$300	$400
$30,000.01–$50,000	$120	NA	$300[4]	$400
$50,000.01–$100,000	$150	NA	$300[4]	$500
$100,000.01–$500,000	$200	NA	$300[4]	$750
$500,000.01–$5,000,000	$250	NA	$300[4]	$1000
Over $5,000,000	$300	NA	$300[4]	$1500

[1]Simplified Arbitration (Without Hearing)
[2]One Arbitrator (Per Hearing Session)
[3]Three or more Arbitrators (Per Hearing Session)
[4]Prehearing Conferences Only

Industry Claimant

Amount in Dispute (Exclusive of Interest and Expenses)	Claim Filing Fee	Hearing Session Deposit		
		Simplified[1]	One Arbitrator[2]	Three + Arbitrators[3]
$0.01–$1,000	$500	$75	$300	NA
$1000.01–$2,500	$500	$75	$300	NA
$2,500.01–$5,000	$500	$75	$300	NA
$5,000.01–$10,000	$500	$75	$300	NA
$10,000.01–$30,000	$500	NA	$300	$400

259

$30,000.01–$50,000	$500	NA	$300[4]	$400
$50,000.01–$100,000	$500	NA	$300[4]	$500
$100,000.01–$500,000	$500	NA	$300[4]	$750
$500,000.01–$5,000,000	$500	NA	$300[4]	$1000
Over $5,000,000	$500	NA	$300[4]	$1500

[1]Simplified Arbitration (Without Hearing)
[2]One Arbitrator (Per Hearing Session)
[3]Three or more Arbitrators (Per Hearing Session)
[4]Prehearing Conferences Only

[Amended effective October 1, 1984; July 1, 1987; April 1, 1988; May 10, 1989, June 1, 1990.]

• Resolution of the Board of Governors

¶3744   Failure to Act Under Provisions of Code of Arbitration Procedure

It may be deemed conduct inconsistent with just and equitable principles of trade and a violation of Article III Section 1 of the Rules of Fair Practice for a member or a person associated with a member to fail to submit a dispute for arbitration under the NASD Code of Arbitration Procedure as required by that Code, to fail to appear or to produce any document in his possession or control as directed pursuant to provisions of the NASD Code of Arbitration Procedure, or to fail to honor an award of arbitrators properly rendered pursuant to the Uniform Code of Arbitration under the auspices of the National Association of Securities Dealers, Inc., the New York, American, Boston, Cincinnati, Midwest, Pacific, or Philadelphia Stock Exchanges, the Chicago Board Options Exchange, the Municipal Securities Rule Making Board, or pursuant to the rules applicable to the arbitration of securities disputes before the American Arbitration Association, where a timely motion has not been made to vacate or modify such award pursuant to applicable law.

All awards shall be honored by a cash payment to the prevailing, party of the exact dollar amount stated in the award. Awards may not be honored by crediting the prevailing party's account with the dollar amount of the award, unless authorized by the express terms of the award or consented to in writing by the parties. Awards shall be honored upon receipt thereof, or within such other time period as may be prescribed by the award.

Action by members requiring associated persons to waive the arbitration of disputes contrary to the provisions of the Code of Arbitration Procedure shall constitute conduct that is inconsistent with just and equitable principles of trade and a violation of Article III, Section 1 of the Rules of Fair Practice.

(Resolution adopted effective May 1,1973 and amended July 1,1987; May 7,1991.)

• Selected NASD Notices to Members

87–55 Amendments to NASD Code of Arbitration Procedure effective July 1,1987.

(August 14,1987)

88–14 Additional Arbitration Filing Fee and Advertising Service Charge.

(February 10, 1988)

¶3746   Schedule of Fees for Industry and Clearing Controversies

Sec. 44. (a) At the time of filing a Claim, Counterclaim, Third-Party Claim or a Cross-Claim in an industry or clearing controversy which is required to be submitted to arbitration before the Association as set forth in Section 8, above, a party shall pay a non-refundable filing fee and shall remit a hearing session deposit to the Association in the amounts indicated in the schedule below unless such fee or deposit is specifically waived by the Director of Arbitration.

Where multiple hearing sessions are required, the arbitrator(s) may require any of the parties to make additional hearing deposits for each additional hearing session. In no event shall the amount deposited by all parties per hearing session exceed the amount of the largest initial hearing deposit made by any party under the schedule below.

(b) A hearing session is any meeting between the parties and the arbitrator(s), including a pre-hearing conference with an arbitrator, which lasts four (4) hours or less. The forum fee for a pre-hearing conference with an arbitrator shall be the amount set forth in the schedule below as a hearing session deposit for a hearing with a single arbitrator.

(c) The arbitrators, in their award, shall determine the amount chargeable to the parties as forum fees and shall determine who shall pay such forum fees. Forum fees chargeable to the parties shall be assessed on a per hearing session basis and the aggregate for each hearing session may equal but shall not exceed the amount of the largest initial hearing deposit deposited by any party, except in a case where claims have been joined subsequent to filing in which case hearing session fees shall be computed as provided in paragraph (d). The arbitrator(s) may determine in the award that a party shall reimburse to another party any non-refundable filing fee it has paid. Amounts deposited by a party shall be applied against forum fees, if any. In addition to forum fees, the arbitrator(s) may determine in the award the amount of costs incurred pursuant to Sections 30, 32, 33, and 37 and, unless applicable law directs otherwise other costs and expenses of the parties and arbitrator(s) which are within the scope of the agreement of the parties. The arbitrator(s) shall determine by whom such costs shall be borne. If the hearing session fees are not assessed against a party who had made a hearing deposit, the hearing deposit will be refunded unless the arbitrators determine otherwise.

(d) For claims filed separately which are subsequently joined or consolidated under Section 25(d) of this Code, the hearing deposit and forum fees assessable per hearing session after joinder or consolidation shall be based on the cumulative amount in dispute. The arbitrator(s) shall determine by whom such fees shall be borne.

(e) If the dispute, claim, or controversy does not involve, disclose or specify a money claim the non-refundable filing fee will be $250 and the hearing session deposit to be deposited by a party shall be $600, or such greater or lesser amount as the Director of Arbitration or the panel of arbitrators may require, but shall not exceed $1,000.

261

(f) The Association shall retain the total initial amount deposited as hearing session deposits by all the parties in any matter submitted and settled or withdrawn within eight business days of the first scheduled hearing session other than a prehearing conference.

(g) Any matter submitted and thereafter settled or withdrawn subsequent to the commencement of the first hearing session, including a pre-hearing conference with an arbitrator, shall be subject to an assessment of forum fees and costs incurred pursuant to Sections 30, 32, 33, and 37 based on hearing sessions held and scheduled within eight business days after the Association receives notice that the matter has been settled or withdrawn. The arbitrator(s) shall determine by whom such fees and costs shall be borne.

(h) In each industry or clearing controversy which is required to be submitted to arbitration before the Association as set forth in Section 8, above, requiring expedited hearings, a non-refundable surcharge of $2,500 shall be paid by all Claimants, collectively, and a non-refundable surcharge of $2,500 shall be paid by all Respondents, collectively. These surcharge fees shall be in addition to all other non-refundable filing fees, hearing deposits, or costs which may be required.

Schedule of Fees

Amount in Dispute (Exclusive of Interest and Expenses)	Claim Filing Fee	Hearing Session Deposit		
		Simplified[1]	One Arbitrator[2]	Three Abitrators[3]
$.01–$1,000	$500	$75	$300	NA
$1000.01–$2500	$500	$75	$300	NA
$2,500.01–$5,000	$500	$75	$300	NA
$5,000.01–10,000	$500	$75	$300	NA
$10,000.01–$30,000	$500	NA	$300	$ 600
$30,000.01–$50,000	$500	NA	$300[4]	$ 600
$50,000.01–$100,000	$500	NA	$300[4]	$ 600
$100,000.01–$500,000	$500	NA	$300[4]	$ 750
$500,000.01–$5,000,000	$500	NA	$300[4]	$1000
Over $5,000,000	$500	NA	$300[4]	$1500

[1]Simplified Arbitration (Without Hearing)
[2]One Arbitrator (Per Hearing Session)
[3]Three or more Arbitrators (Per Hearing Session)
[4]Prehearing Conferences Only

[Section 45 added effective May 10, 1989; amended effective June 1, 1990.]

• Selected NASD Notice to Members

90–47 Amendments to Code of Arbitration Procedure

(July 1990)

SECTION SIX

FRANCHISES

A franchise is the purchase of the right to conduct business using certain trademarks that have already been established by a parent company. The parent company, or franchisor, sells the rights to use these trademarks to the individual business owner, or franchisee. Examples of franchises include fast food restaurants, hair salons, home decorating businesses and sports/fitness enterprises.

A franchise may provide the opportunity for an individual who wants to pursue a business with a way to fulfill his or her dreams. But before investing in a franchise, potential franchisees should carefully scrutinize the franchise agreement.

Many franchisors make misrepresentations to potential franchisees regarding their opportunities for earnings or sales. Likewise, misrepresentations may be made with regard to what territory the franchisee will be guaranteed as part of the business, or the success rate that other franchisees have had with similar businesses. In addition, franchisors may tell potential franchisees that they will be independent business owners under the franchise agreement, when in fact the franchise agreement requires the franchisee to adhere to a multitude of franchisor-specified rules and regulations. Finally, the cost of investing in a franchise may be substantial. The more established and well-known the parent company, the greater the investment that will be required of the potential franchisee.

Before investing in any franchise, you should consider factors including:

1. Does the franchise agreement require payment of a certain amount on a monthly or annual basis to the franchisor, regardless of actual profits?

2. Does the franchisor require adherence to certain rules and regulations; if so, does the franchisor impose any

penalties for non-adherence? Will such rules and regulations infringe upon your right to conduct business in a manner that you see fit?

3. What arrangements will be made by the franchisor to assist you financially during the start-up time for your franchise? What assistance will the franchisor provide if your franchise goes through "slow" periods? Does the franchisor expect specific returns from the franchise within a specified amount of time?

While franchises are marketed as business opportunities, many franchisors grant franchisees only the rights they would receive as employees, while imposing upon them all of the liabilities associated with being an independent business owner. Franchisors may endeavor to convince individuals to purchase a franchise rather than start their own business by citing the "safety" of the investment in a franchise as opposed to the "risk" of commencing an individually owned business. Potential investors in franchises should carefully investigate such representations, since some studies have shown that franchised businesses actually have a greater risk of failure than businesses that are individually owned.

Before entering into any franchise agreement, obtain all promises that are made by the franchisor in writing. If the franchisor refuses to reduce a representation to writing, this should alert the potential franchisee to the possibility that the franchisor cannot deliver on the promise. Before entering into a franchise agreement, the potential franchisee should have the franchise agreement reviewed by their own legal counsel. Remember, the franchisor is in all probability a large, powerful corporation with hundreds of attorneys at its disposal. The franchisor wants an agreement that best protects its rights and its ability to obtain profits from the franchise. Review of the franchise agreement by the potential franchisee's own lawyer may alert the franchisee to provisions in the agreement that could be potentially detrimental to his or her interests.

If you have purchased a franchise based on misrepresentations that were made by the franchisor, and you believe that you have sustained financial damage as a result, you may wish to consult with an attorney. You should plan to provide your attorney with documentation including all information given to you by the franchisor, the franchise agreement, and financial information for both you and the franchise. As with most claims, you must start your case within the statute of limitations. By consulting with an attorney, you can best protect your rights.

SECTION SEVEN

DISCRIMINATION

Discrimination may occur in many contexts. Individuals have been discriminated against based on classifications including age, gender, gender preference, physical characteristics, skin color, and religious beliefs. Legal action seeking redress for discriminatory acts often arises out of conduct that occurs in the workplace. Examples of potentially actionable claims include:

1. Loss of a deserved promotion or salary increase

2. Employer creates or condones work environment so hostile that employee has no other alternative than to terminate employment

3. Employer engages in specific patterns or practices applicable only to specific groups of employees

4. Career advancement or continued employment conditioned on compliance with employer demands that are unrelated to job duties

Individuals who believe that they have been discriminated against may be able to pursue legal action on a number of grounds. Federal and state law may provide remedies for some claims. In addition, many states permit individuals to bring lawsuits against the person or entity that engaged in the discriminatory conduct.

As in virtually all claims, legal action must be started within a specified amount of time. These time limits vary from state to state. If you believe that you have been injured due to discriminatory conduct, you should seek the advice of an attorney immediately to ensure that your rights are protected.

In order to substantiate a discrimination claim, the injured person should be able to describe the alleged discriminatory conduct with specificity—what was said or done, at what times, in what locations, on how many occasions. Written complaints to supervisory personnel may help to substantiate an injured person's claims. Co-workers may have witnessed or been subjected to the discriminatory conduct, and may thus furnish valuable testimony. Documents such as employee handbooks and company records may likewise provide important information regarding a particular company's approach to handling discriminatory conduct in the workplace. Information pertaining to the job description, educational background, and salary history of the injured person are also important, because they establish what damages have been sustained.

Individuals who have been discriminated against sometimes decline to pursue their legal rights due to fear of further retaliation by their employer or supervisor. But employers are not permitted to take retaliatory action against employees who seek enforcement of their legal rights. Filing a discrimination claim does not ensure that an employee will not be fired or demoted, however. If the employer or supervisor can show a reason for the adverse action that is unrelated to the discrimination claim—for example, poor job performance—the adverse action is unlikely to be regarded as retaliatory.

SECTION EIGHT

DAMAGES

The term "damages" in the context of a legal case ordinarily refers to the total amount of money that will be given to the injured person to make him or her "whole" again after an injury of any kind. Such damages can be divided into two categories—general damages and special damages.

General damages compensate people who have sustained physical or emotional injuries for the past and future pain and suffering associated with those injuries, as well as for any permanent effects associated with those injuries. If you were married at the time of your injury, your spouse may also be entitled to damages for his or her loss of your services due to your injury. General damages are ordinarily established through the testimony of the injured person, the testimony and records of medical care providers, and other expert witnesses. Determining how much to award in general damages is a somewhat subjective process, because every injury is different, and every injured person is affected in a different way.

Special damages reimburse people who have sustained any sort of injury for specific losses that can be documented, such as lost earnings, medical expenses, business losses, and repair bills. Special damages are ordinarily established through documents such as bills, tax returns, canceled checks, payroll records, receipts, and other documents that quantify the value of particular items. Direct testimony of the injured person, the person who provided particular goods or services, and expert economists may also assist in the establishment of special damages.

In addition to general and special damages, which focus on restoring the injured person to the same place where he or she was before the injury, punitive damages are sometimes awarded. The purpose of punitive damages is to punish the defendant, not to make the plaintiff whole again. Punitive damages can only be awarded where the injured person has shown that the defendant's conduct was reckless, malicious, or otherwise in flagrant disregard of the injured person's rights.

If your case is tried in court and it is determined that you are entitled to recover, the jury will award separate amounts to you for your past pain and suffering, future pain and suffering, spouse's claim (if any), lost earnings, out of pocket expenses, and punitive damages (if appropriate). If you settle your case out of court, however, you will probably be offered a lump sum amount, which is intended to encompass all elements of your damages.

SECTION NINE

LAWYERS

SELECTING AND HIRING A LAWYER

Qualifications

When selecting your lawyer, you should consider numerous criteria. First, you should consider whether the lawyer possesses substantial expertise in the type of law involved in your case. You should take into consideration that a lawyer who specializes may be more experienced than a lawyer who practices in all areas of law. A lawyer who specializes deals with cases like yours every working day. Specialized lawyers have a greater awareness of the techniques used by their opponents to slow down and complicate the resolution of cases. Specialized lawyers' relationships with opposing counsel may also be an asset in terms of early resolution of a case by settlement, where appropriate. A lawyer who specializes may have greater trial experience than a general practitioner.

A specialized lawyer will have tried many of the different aspects of cases like yours, whereas a general practitioner may never have tried such a case. A specialized lawyer will also have a greater knowledge of different expert witnesses available to testify in regard to a particular situation, and will have a greater familiarity with the terminology critical to the case. A specialized lawyer will have a clear idea of what to expect with regard to pre-trial discovery procedures. A non-specialized lawyer may do only one or two such proceedings in an entire year, whereas a specialized lawyer handles several of such proceedings in the course of a week. The specialized lawyer will be able to anticipate what questions may be asked of the client, and therefore will better prepare the client to answer such questions. The specialized lawyer will also have a greater understanding of how to handle the extensive paperwork associated with most cases, whereas a general practitioner may not have the time or resources to efficiently process such documents.

Also consider the size of the lawyer's office and what types of resources are available to the office when determining whether a particular lawyer is appropriate for your needs. A lawyer who practices alone may not have the time or financial resources required to handle a particular type of case. On the other hand, a lawyer who works as a team with other lawyers, paralegals and support staff may be able to work more productively on your case, thus offering you better results.

Fees and expenses

When you need a lawyer to help you recover for damages you have sustained due to bodily injuries, investment or business losses, or discriminatory acts, you have two choices. You can hire a lawyer by the hour. Many lawyers charge anywhere from $100.00 to $400.00 per hour. Such costs may be a barrier to hiring a lawyer on an hourly basis.

Your other option is to find a lawyer who works on a contingent fee basis—in other words, a lawyer who charges no legal fee until and unless you win your case. Such arrangements may be preferable to the substantial cost of retaining a lawyer on an hourly basis. In addition, you may feel more confident in a lawyer who invests time and money to fight for your case. It is unlikely that a lawyer would accept a case on a contingent fee basis if he or she does not believe in the case.

When you have your initial meeting with your lawyer, you may wish to have the fee agreement put in writing. By reducing the fee arrangement to writing, both you and your lawyer prevent the chance of a disagreement or misunderstanding later in the case.

The law in most states requires the client to be responsible for all expenses the lawyer incurs to build up the case. Many lawyers charge in advance for expenses they incur in investigating and building a case, which can add up to hundreds or even thousands of dollars. These expenses include the costs of obtaining medical, financial, and employment records, private investigators, expert witnesses, and court costs. Do not be afraid to see a lawyer because the law requires you to be responsible for these expenses. Some law firms will advance all of the money required to build up your case. The money that the lawyer has advanced to build up your case will be deducted from the settlement. Typically, such expenses are small compared to the amount that can be collected on your case.

WHAT IS A RETAINER AGREEMENT?

A retainer agreement is an agreement between the client and the lawyer. This agreement may include information on how much and when the lawyer will be paid, as well as when and who will pay for the expenses associated with investigation and litigation of the case. Most agreements in cases seeking to recover for personal or financial injuries call for the lawyer to collect a fee only if the case is settled or won in court. A percentage of the amount settled for or won is paid to the lawyer. The agreement may also provide for what happens if the client decides to change lawyers. Further, a retainer agreement may contain the client's authorization for the law firm to investigate the claim, and may permit the lawyer to stop working on the case if the lawyer discovers that there is no valid claim.

The agreement is required by law in some states. In other states, such agreements are optional. It is good business, however, for both the lawyer and client to insist on a written agreement.

YOUR RELATIONSHIP WITH YOUR LAWYER

Your relationship with your lawyer is confidential. Communications between you and your lawyer are ordinarily private and privileged. This means that your lawyer cannot reveal information that you tell him or her without your consent.

The lawyer you retain should be someone you can trust. In order to best serve you, your lawyer needs to know everything about your case, even details that are embarrassing or potentially damaging to your case.

If you do not have the utmost of faith in a lawyer's abilities, then you should not be represented by that lawyer. In the course of settling or litigating a claim, your lawyer will give you advice which your lawyer will offer with your best interests in mind. If you feel that you cannot trust your lawyer, then you will not trust your lawyer's advice. This situation can be avoided if you carefully consider your feelings when choosing your lawyer.

A lawyer is obligated to represent each and every client to the best of his or her abilities. As a professional, your lawyer should take pride in the representation that he or she offers. Further, your lawyer should be responsive to your needs regarding your case.

Your lawyer is an advocate for your claim. It is unlikely that he or she will cheat you, particularly if the lawyer represents many people with claims like yours. If such a lawyer cheated just one client, the lawyer's reputation could be ruined. A lawyer foolish enough to accept a "payoff" from the other side could lose his or her license to practice law. It is unlikely that a lawyer would risk his or her career for just one case.

While it is preferable to find a lawyer with whom you are comfortable at the start, and stay with that lawyer throughout your case, circumstances may arise under which you may elect to change attorneys. Under such circumstances, your original lawyer will be entitled to compensation for the work he or she performed on your case. This money must be paid out of the attorney's fee that your new lawyer collects when the case reaches judgment or settlement, unless you already made payment arrangements with your original lawyer.

Transferring a case from one lawyer to another can be a time-consuming process. Sometimes the lawyers will argue about the what share of the fee each should receive. Your new lawyer may require time to review and understand your case. Such matters may slow down the resolution of your case.

CAN YOUR LAWYER GIVE YOU A CASH ADVANCE?

Even though your lawyer may want to assist you in putting your life back together after a personal injury or a financial loss, he or she is legally forbidden from providing such help in the form of a cash advance on the proceeds of your settlement. One reason underlying this prohibition is that if a lawyer advanced you cash from your settlement, the lawyer might advise you to settle early, considering his or her own self-interest above your welfare.

The law sets strict ethical guidelines that govern relations between attorneys and their clients. If your lawyer violates these standards, he or she could be barred or suspended from practicing law. No reputable lawyer would risk his or her career for the sake of one client. Therefore, a lawyer's willingness to give you a cash advance on your settlement should alert you to the possibility that the lawyer is not serving your best interests.

HOW TO BE A GOOD CLIENT

You can help your lawyer in many ways:

1. Retain a lawyer experienced with your type of case.

2. Keep all scheduled appointments. If you wish to speak with the lawyer in person, call to make an appointment. Do not go to the lawyer's office without an appointment.

3. Keep detailed notes of your problems and questions so that you can review them with your lawyer.

4. Do not ask a lawyer to give a cash advance.

5. Give your lawyer a reasonable time to return your phone calls. Lawyers are often out of their offices, and thus are not always available to return phone calls immediately.

6. Be completely honest with your lawyer. Tell your lawyer everything about your claim, no matter how insignificant or embarrassing. If you lie to your lawyer or do not tell your lawyer about a potential problem with your case, your lawyer will be at a disadvantage if the problem comes up. Lawyers are used to problems and can work with you to overcome them as long as they know about the problems in advance.

7. Promptly respond to any requests your lawyer makes. For example, if your lawyer asks for copies of your medical bills, he or she has a reason for doing so, and that reason relates to your case. By quickly giving your lawyer the information he or she asks for, you can help to advance your case.

8. Tell the lawyer if you are unhappy. Lawyers need clients, and want to keep them satisfied. If you are unhappy, your lawyer needs to know why so that he or she can better serve you.

9. Remember that your lawyer wants to get the largest possible amount that is fair to compensate you. Sometimes this can take a long time. Your lawyer will appreciate your patience while he or she is working to get you the maximum amount possible.

QUESTIONS YOUR LAWYER WILL ASK

When you first meet with your lawyer, you will be asked many questions. These are aimed at getting the information needed to investigate and prepare your claim. Your attorney can not afford to be surprised later about an important piece of information. The following is a list of common questions asked by lawyers of their clients:

1. Name

2. Home address

3. Phone number

4. Age

5. Social Security Number

6. Marital status

7. Spouse's name

8. Age of spouse

9. Children's names and ages

10. Work address

11. Work phone number

12. Other phone numbers to reach you

13. List of all persons living in household and ages and if they are dependent on you

14. Names of any individuals, including representatives of the defendant or its insurance company, with whom you have already discussed your claim.

15. Copies of any documents that are pertinent to your claim.

16. Describe the state of your health and your financial circumstances prior to the events giving rise to your claim.

17. Provide information about your job title, duties performed, rate of pay, and hours worked prior to the incident giving rise to your claim.

18. Provide documentation of any loss of earnings that you are seeking to recover.

19. Name any witnesses to events pertinent to your claim.

20. Describe any physical problems that have arisen due to your claim.

21. Describe any collateral sources that you have received for—example, workers' compensation, unemployment compensation, no-fault benefits, disability insurance, and welfare benefits all constitute collateral sources.

22. List all expenses that you believe have been incurred as a result of your claim.

23. List all experts with whom you have consulted—such as doctors, economists, accountants, etc.

WHAT IS INVOLVED IN THE CLAIMS PROCESS?

CLAIMS ADJUSTERS

After an accident or injury occurs, a representative of the other side may contact you. This representative is generally a claims adjuster for an insurance company. The adjuster's job is to investigate the circumstances surrounding your injury. The adjuster's objective is to minimize the amount of money that the insurance company will have to pay to settle the case. Once the case is settled, it can never be reopened. Therefore, the adjuster wants to settle the case quickly, and for the smallest amount of money possible.

Insurance adjusters also locate witnesses, obtain photographs of accident scenes, and obtain reports filed by police or other agencies. The adjuster may also seek to obtain information about the medical treatment that you have undergone. With this information, the adjuster will evaluate the claim and arrive at an amount that he or she is willing to offer to you in settlement of your claim.

In cases where injuries have been sustained as a result of accidents, the adjuster will frequently call shortly after the accident. The adjuster may offer to come to your home or hospital room to discuss the claim. The adjuster may express concern for your situation, and offer to provide money to assist you with your immediate needs.

You should beware of dealing with adjusters under these circumstances. The adjuster may take advantage of your vulnerability following an injury in order to achieve his or her goal of a fast settlement for a minimal amount of money.

The insurance adjuster may also seek to visit your home or hospital room to obtain your statement about the accident. The adjuster may also contact you by telephone in an effort to obtain such a statement.

Individuals who have sustained injuries are often confused about what information they are required to provide in order to protect their rights. The insurance adjuster may try to take advantage of such confusion. For example, the adjuster may say that your claim cannot be processed without your statement.

If you have been injured in an accident, you are not required to speak with the insurance adjuster who represents the other side. You must report the accident to your own insurance company and provide your own insurance company with a statement of the facts. You have no obligation to assist the other side's insurance company in developing its case.

If you have already given a statement to an insurance adjuster—whether from your own insurance company or from the insurance company for the other side—you are entitled to receive a copy of this statement. If the adjuster fails to provide a copy to you, you should request a copy in writing from the adjuster. Such statements are important because they reflect your perceptions of an accident immediately after it occurred, when details such as weather and roadway conditions, vehicle locations, witnesses, and actions taken by all parties involved are fresh in your mind. Further, such statements are often important, because they are given at a time when the people involved in the accident have not yet had an opportunity to reflect on the facts of the accident with self-interest in mind.

MEDICAL AUTHORIZATIONS

If you have been injured, there is nothing that you can do to prevent an insurance adjuster from speaking with witnesses, police officers, and other individuals who might have knowledge about the incident that caused your injuries. Likewise, there is nothing that you can do to prevent the adjuster from obtaining documents such as police reports which are public records. There is one source of information, however, that you can control. This source is your medical records.

The adjuster may ask you to sign an authorization form allowing him or her to obtain copies of your medical records. It is highly inadvisable to sign such a form without seeking legal advice. Adjusters will generally seek a very broad authorization. A broadly worded authorization will allow the adjuster to inquire into any and all of your medical records, including those that existed prior to the injury giving rise to your claim. If you sign such an authorization, the adjuster will be able to browse freely among all of your medical records, even if they bear no relationship to your claim. The adjuster may then use any information obtained through such records in an effort to try and minimize the value of your case. For example, if you injure your knee in a motor vehicle accident and subsequently give the adjuster an unlimited medical authorization, the adjuster might look in your medical records and find that you had injured the same knee several years ago. The adjuster might then argue that your injuries are related to your previous injury, rather than to the accident from which your present claim arises.

SETTLEMENT OFFERS

The adjuster may elect to offer you a settlement. If you are not represented by an attorney, it is unlikely that you will know whether the adjuster's offer is fair. If you settle a case without seeking legal advice, you may be cheating yourself out of thousands of dollars. The adjuster is highly experienced in handling claims such as yours, whereas you have probably never been involved in such a matter before. By consulting an attorney who is experienced in handling cases such as yours, you can help to put yourself on an even footing with the adjuster, and work toward a settlement which fairly reflects the value of your case.

Once you have hired an attorney, the attorney will gather information about your case. Much of the information that your attorney gathers will be the same type of information that the adjuster obtains—witness statements, police reports, photographs, and medical records. Your attorney may provide the adjuster with information that will enable the adjuster to evaluate your claim, but will probably restrict the adjuster's access to other records.

Once your doctors have concluded that you have reached a point of maximum improvement from your injuries, your attorney may endeavor to settle your claim. Your attorney may prepare a demand letter or settlement package to send to the adjuster. Information contained in a demand letter or settlement package might include a summary of the accident and the injuries that you sustained, medical records documenting your treatment history and the permanent effects associated with your injuries, medical bills, photographs of your injuries and/or of the accident scene, and any other information that your attorney believes is important to your case. Your attorney may also specify an amount of money that he or she believes would be appropriate to settle your case. Such settlement demands generally provide the insurance company with a time frame in which to respond with a settlement offer; if settlement negotiations are not initiated within that time, the attorney may start a lawsuit to show the insurance company that he or she is serious about obtaining a fair amount for your injuries.

The insurance company may respond to your attorney's settlement demand. It is unlikely, however, that the attorney's demand will be met. It is much more likely that the insurance company will make a counteroffer, and the process of negotiating between your attorney and the insurance company will begin. On some occasions, both sides will be able to reach a compromise that reflects a fair value for your case. In other instances, however, the insurance company will refuse, even after extended negotiations, to offer a fair settlement. In such instances, the attorney will have no alternative but to initiate a lawsuit to further pursue your claim.

RELEASES

In the event that a mutually satisfactory settlement is reached, your attorney will provide you with a release form to sign. Releases ordinarily provide that in exchange for a particular sum of money, the injured person ends any and all claims that he or she may have against the person who is responsible for causing his or her injuries. Signing a release means that you are ending your case. Once you have signed a release and given it to the insurance company, you cannot change your mind and decide that you want more money. Even if you discover that your injuries are much more serious than you thought, you cannot re-open the case in an effort to recover more money.

INSURANCE COMPANY BAD FAITH

On occasion, the facts surrounding a case will clearly demonstrate the injured person's entitlement to a substantial recovery. If the amount of insurance coverage available is far less than the value of the injuries, the insurance company has an obligation to quickly resolve the claim by payment of the full policy limits. If the insurance company fails to do so, such failure may be regarded as bad faith. If the insurance company is found to be in bad faith, the insurance company may be required to pay the injured person over and about its policy limits. If your attorney believes that the insurance company is acting in bad faith with regard to its refusal to settle your claim, he or she will take the necessary steps to preserve your rights to recover directly against the insurance company.

WHERE TO COMPLAIN ABOUT INSURANCE COMPANIES

ALABAMA: Alabama Insurance Department; 135 South Union Street; Montgomery, AL 36130-3401; 205/269-3550

ALASKA: Alaska Insurance Department; 800 East Diamond, Suite 560; Anchorage, AK 99515; 907/349-1230

ARIZONA: Arizona Insurance Department; Consumer Affairs and Investigation; 3030 North Third Street; Phoenix, AZ 85012; 602/255-4783

ARKANSAS: Arkansas Insurance Department; Consumer Service Division; 400 University Tower Building; 12th and University Streets; Little Rock, AR 72204; 501/686-2945

CALIFORNIA: California Insurance Department; Consumer Services Division; Claims Service Bureau; 3450 Wilshire Boulevard; Los Angeles, CA 90010; 800/927-4357 (within state)

COLORADO: Colorado Insurance Division; 1560 Broadway, Suite 850; Denver, CO 80202; 303/894-7499

CONNECTICUT: Connecticut Insurance Department; Post Office Box 816; Hartford, CT 06142-0816; 203/297-3800

DELAWARE: Delaware Insurance Department; 841 Silver Lake Boulevard; Dover, DE 19901; 302/739-4251

DISTRICT OF COLUMBIA:	District of Columbia Insurance Department; 613 G Street, NW Room 619; Post Office Box 37200; Washington, DC 20013-7200; 202/727-8017
FLORIDA:	Florida Department of Insurance; State Capitol; Plaza Level Eleven; 200 East Gaines Street; Tallahassee, FL 32399-0300; 800/342-2762 (within state); 904/922-3100
GEORGIA:	Georgia Insurance Department; 2 Martin Luther King, Jr. Drive; Room 716, West Tower; Atlanta, GA 30334; 404/656-2056
HAWAII:	Hawaii Department of Commerce and Consumer Affairs; Insurance Division; Post Office Box 3614; Honolulu, HI 96811-3614; 808/586-2790
IDAHO:	Idaho Insurance Department; Public Service Department; 500 South 10th Street; Boise, ID 83720; 208/334-4250
ILLINOIS:	Illinois Insurance Department; 320 West Washington Street, 4th Floor; Springfield, IL 62767; 217/782-4515
INDIANA:	Indiana Insurance Department; 311 West Washington Street, Suite 300; Indianapolis, IN 46204; 317/232-2395
IOWA:	Iowa Insurance Division; Lucas State Office Building; East 12th and Grand Streets; Des Moines, IA 50319; 515/281-5705
KANSAS:	Kansas Insurance Department; 420 Southwest 9th Street; Topeka, KS 66612-1678; 913/296-3071

KENTUCKY:	Kentucky Insurance Department; 229 West Main Street; Post Office Box 517; Frankfort, KY 40602; 502/564-3630
LOUISIANA:	Louisiana Insurance Department; Post Office Box 94214; Baton Rouge, LA 70804-9214; 504/342-5900
MAINE:	Maine Bureau of insurance; Consumer Division; State House, Station #34; Augusta, ME 04333; 207/582-8707
MARYLAND:	Maryland Insurance Department; Complaints and Investigation Unit; 501 St. Paul Place; Baltimore, MD 21202-2272; 410/333-6300
MASSACHUSETTS:	Massachusetts Insurance Division; Consumer Services Section; 280 Friend Street; Boston, MA 02114; 617/727-7189
MICHIGAN:	Michigan Insurance Department; Post Office Box 30220; Lansing, MI 48909; 517/373-0220
MINNESOTA:	Minnesota Insurance Department; Department of Commerce; 133 East 7th Street; St. Paul, MN 55101; 612/296-4026
MISSISSIPPI:	Mississippi Insurance Department; Consumer Assistance Division; Post Office Box 79; Jackson, MS 39205; 601/359-3569
MISSOURI:	Missouri Division of Insurance; Consumer Services Section; Post Office Box 690; Jefferson City, MO 65102-0690; 314/751-2640
MONTANA:	Montana Insurance Department; 126 North Sanders, Room 270; Post Office

	Box 4009; Helena, MT 59604; 800/332-6148 (within state); 406/444-2040
NEBRASKA:	Nebraska Insurance Department; Terminal Building; 941 0 Street, Suite 400; Lincoln, NE 68508; 402/471-2201
NEVADA:	Nevada Department of Commerce; Insurance Division, Consumer Section; 1665 Hot Springs Road; Capitol Complex, Suite 152; Carson City, NV 89701; 702/687-4270
NEW HAMPSHIRE:	New Hampshire Insurance Department; Life and Health Division; 169 Manchester Street; Concord, NH 03301-5151; 603/271-2261
NEW JERSEY:	New Jersey Insurance Department; 20 West State Street; Roebling Building; Trenton, NJ 08625-0325; 609/292-4757
NEW MEXICO:	New Mexico Insurance Department; Post Office Drawer 1269; Santa Fe, NM 87504-1269; 505/827-4500
NEW YORK:	New York Insurance Department; 160 West Broadway; New York, NY 10013; 212/602-0203 (New York City); 800/342-3736 (within state, outside NYC)
NORTH CAROLINA:	North Carolina Insurance Department; Consumer Services; Post Office Box 26387; Raleigh, NC 27611; 919/733-2004
NORTH DAKOTA:	North Dakota Insurance Department; Capitol Building, 5th Floor; 600 East Boulevard Avenue; Bismarck, ND 58505-0320; 701/224-2440

OHIO:	Ohio Insurance Department; Consumer Services Division; 2100 Stella Court; Columbus, OH 43266-0566; 614/644-2673
OKLAHOMA:	Oklahoma Insurance Department; Post Office Box 53408; Oklahoma City, OK 73152-3408; 405/521-2828
OREGON:	Oregon Department of Insurance and Finance; Insurance Division/Consumer Advocate; 440-7 Labor and Industry Building; Salem, OR 97310; 503/378-4484
PENNSYLVANIA:	Pennsylvania Insurance Department; 1321 Strawberry Square; Harrisburg, PA 17120; 717/787-2317
RHODE ISLAND:	Rhode Island Insurance Division; 233 Richmond Street, Suite 233; Providence, RI 02903-4233; 401/277-2223
SOUTH CAROLINA:	South Carolina Insurance Department; Post Office Box 100105; Columbia, SC 29202-3105; 803/737-6140
SOUTH DAKOTA:	South Dakota Insurance Department; Consumer Assistance Section; 500 East Central; Pierre, SD 57501-3940; 605/773-3563
TENNESSEE:	Tennessee Department of Commerce and Insurance; Policyholders Service Section; 500 James Robertson Parkway, 4th Floor; Nashville, TN 37243-0582; 800/342-4029 (within state); 615/741-4955
TEXAS:	Texas Board of Insurance Complaints Division; 1110 San Jacinto Boulevard; Austin, TX 78701-1998; 512/463-6501

UTAH:	Utah Insurance Department; Consumer Services; 3110 State Office Building; Salt Lake City, UT 84114; 801/530-6400
VERMONT:	Vermont Department of Insurance and Banking; Consumer Complaint Division; 120 State Street; Montpelier, VT 05602; 802/828-3301
VIRGINIA:	Virginia Insurance Department; Consumer Services Division; 700 Jefferson Building; Post Office Box 1157; Richmond, VA 23209; 804/786-7691
WASHINGTON:	Washington Insurance Department; Insurance Building; Post Office Box 40255; Olympia, WA 98504-0255; 800/562-6900 (within state); 206/753-7300
WEST VIRGINIA:	West Virginia Insurance Department; Post Office Box 50540; 2019 Washington Street, East; Charleston, WV 25305-0540; 304/558-3386
WISCONSIN:	Wisconsin Insurance Department; Complaints Department; Post Office Box 7873; Madison, WI 53707; 608/266-0103
WYOMING:	Wyoming Insurance Department; Herschler Building; 122 West 25th Street; Cheyenne, WY 82002; 307/777-7401

CONSIDERATIONS BEFORE SETTLING ANY CLAIM

HOW MUCH IS YOUR CASE WORTH

The most frequently asked question before a case is won or settled is, "How much is my case worth?" When you first see a lawyer, it is difficult to answer this question. Without development of the pertinent facts surrounding the case, even a "ballpark" figure cannot be stated. In many cases, only a jury can decide how much money you will ultimately receive. Your lawyer needs to know the answers to many questions before giving you an idea of the value of your case. Examples of these questions are listed below:

Questions that apply to all cases:

1. Are you willing to go to court to fight your case?

2. Do you have witnesses who support your claim?

3. Does the opposing party or insurance company prefer to settle or go to court?

4. Will you make a sympathetic witness in court?

5. Is your lawyer known as an experienced lawyer who will fight in court, if needed?

6. How long will it take to schedule a trial in court?

7. How much will it cost to go to court (consider expert witness fees, court costs, and the "time value of money")?

8. How much have juries awarded in the past to other people who have brought cases such as yours?

Questions that apply to cases involving bodily injuries:

1. How did your injuries occur?

2. What kind of injuries did you sustain?

3. Will you need future medical care?

4. Have you followed your doctor's orders for treatment?

5. Did you have any pre-existing injuries or health problems?

6. Did you cause or aggravate your own injuries?

7. Have you sustained any out-of-pocket expenses (such as medical bills, prescriptions, nursing services not covered by insurance) due to your injuries?

8. Have you lost money due to missing time from work?

9. Does your doctor expect your injuries to be permanent?

If your injuries were sustained due to an accident, you should also ask:

10. How did the accident occur?

11. Who was at fault for the accident?

12. Was the accident reported to the police or other authorities?

13. Did you contribute to the accident by violating any laws? For example, in a motor vehicle accident, were you speeding?

If your accident involved a condition that you claim was defective—such as an icy area or a malfunctioning product—you should also ask:

14. Did the person responsible for maintaining the dangerous area or defective product know or have reason

to know that a problem existed <u>before</u> your accident occurred?

Questions that apply to cases involving business or investment losses:

1. What was your financial situation prior to making the transaction that caused your loss?

2. What did you do to investigate the transaction before investing your funds? Was the stockbroker or franchisor your only source of information?

3. Did the stockbroker or franchisor misrepresent any important facts, or make promises that were not delivered?

4. How much money did you invest?

5. How much money did you lose?

If your claim arises out of a transaction involving stock or other securities, you should also ask:

6. Was the investment a suitable one for the broker to sell to you?

7. Did the broker encourage you to make frequent, unnecessary trades?

8. Did the broker make unauthorized trades?

Questions that apply to cases involving discrimination:

1. Did the person or entity that committed the discriminatory act give a justification or pretext for doing so? For example, were "safety reasons" cited to prevent women from obtaining certain jobs?

2. Does the discriminatory person or entity have a history of engaging in similar conduct toward others?

3. Was the discriminatory conduct reported to anyone else at the time that it occurred?

4. What financial losses have you suffered as a result of the discriminatory conduct?

If the discriminatory conduct occurred in your workplace, you should also ask:

5. What sort of work performance did you have prior to being confronted with the discriminatory conduct? Could any aspect of your prior work performance be used as a pretext for such conduct?

Someone who has had a similar case may try to tell you that your claim is worth a certain amount. Such advice is rarely accurate. Since every case and every individual are unique, it is impossible to say that a value that was fair for one person would be fair when applied to someone else. For example, the other person may not have the same severity of an injury as you. It is reasonable to assume that someone with a permanent injury, causing them pain and suffering for the rest of their life, will collect more cash and benefits than a person who has made a complete recovery.

Your lawyer will fight for you with the responsible party or insurance company. Your lawyer will negotiate with the other side to receive their highest offer to settle your case without going to court. Your lawyer will then explain to you the arguments in favor of your case and the opposing side's arguments against your case. Then your lawyer will advise you of his or her opinion concerning the value of your case. You will know how much the other side believes your case to be worth from the settlement offer. You will also have your lawyer's opinion. You can then make your choice to go to trial or to settle out of court.

Remember, no lawyer can tell you how much your case is worth to the penny. If your case is not settled out of court, a jury or judge will decide how much you will receive. The facts of every case are different. Similar cases may have different outcomes. You may receive much more money than you anticipated. In some cases, you might discover that you are entitled to receive less than you thought. More than 90% of all civil cases are settled out of court or before a trial is complete. This is because both sides are apprehensive of the unknown outcome of a trial.

HOW LONG DOES IT TAKE TO RECOVER MONEY ON A CASE

An important factor in determining whether to settle a case or wait for a trial in court is your recovery time. In general, you will receive money at an earlier date if you elect to accept a settlement offer rather than proceed to trial. You can only win or settle a case once. If the case is settled before you realize the full extent of your injuries, it will be too late to go back and recover for these losses.

After you and your lawyer have gathered information about the extent of your injuries or losses, resolution of your claim can take anywhere from a few months to several years. The length of time involved depends on factors including the nature and extent of your injuries or losses; the situation that gives rise to your claim; the evidence that your lawyer can present in support of your position; and the evidence that the other side may possess in opposition to your case.

In some cases, a fair offer to settle will not be made until you pick a jury at your trial. On occasion, no offer to settle will be ever be extended, and you must rely on the jury to decide the value of your case.

SHOULD YOU GO TO COURT OR SETTLE?

With most claims, a time will come when the other side will make an offer to settle your case without going to court. You will then need to decide whether to accept the settlement or wait for a trial.

The advantages of settling your case out of court include the following:

1. You know how much you will receive.

2. You will receive your money now rather than later.

3. You have no risk of losing and getting nothing for your injuries.

4. You will not have to undergo cross-examination in court by the lawyer for the other side.

5. You will not have to pay additional court costs, expert witness fees, and further investigation costs.

6. You will not be surprised by new information that could hurt or ruin your claim.

7. You can put the matter behind you and go on with your life.

8. You will not risk the chance that the defendant or its insurance company will go bankrupt before you win. It is useless to win if you cannot collect.

The disadvantages of settling your case include the following:

1. You can only win or settle one time. You cannot go back and ask for more money if you later find out that you have sustained additional damages, or if your

damages become more serious than they currently appear.

2. A jury could give much more money than the current settlement offer.

3. You will not have your "day in court."

4. You might find new information that adds value to your case.

Most cases settle out of court. This is because the lawyers for both sides know that juries can give a large award, a small award, or no award at all. Trials are expensive for both sides. A lawyer's time in court is worth thousands of dollars each day. Expert witnesses' fees can be immense. The total cost of going to court, combined with the unknown outcome, often makes the decision easy.

In some cases, however, the other side makes an offer that is not fair. Going to court makes sense in these instances. A small offer means little risk to your case.

You should consult with your lawyer and ask his or her advice on settling any claim. Law firms that handle claims such as yours will know the tactics used by the other side, and will know whether a settlement offer is fair.

Lawyers should be willing to go to court when they believe that an offer is unfair. The other side will take advantage of any lawyer who is afraid of court. A good lawyer will fight in court for his or her client's rights and money whenever necessary.

WHAT ARE LIENS AND HOW DO THEY AFFECT SETTLEMENT OF A CASE?

During the course of working on an injured person's claim, a lawyer may become aware of bills that the client owes, such as for medical treatment associated with the client's injuries. If there is no insurance coverage available to pay these bills, and if the client is unable to pay them out of his or her own pocket, the attorney may make arrangements for a lien to be placed against the settlement proceeds. The lien reflects the financial interest of someone else, in this example, a medical care provider, in the settlement proceeds. The amount of the lien will be deducted from the injured person's proceeds before the injured person receives any money. In this example, the lien may be of benefit to the injured person by keeping the unpaid medical bills out of collection, and assuring the medical care providers that their bills will be paid upon settlement of the case.

Another situation where liens can arise is where the injured person has both a Workers' Compensation claim and an action for personal injuries (third party action). When the third party action is settled, the insurance company that provided Workers' Compensation will expect to be reimbursed from the settlement proceeds for any amounts that it has paid for medical expenses and lost earnings. This expectation of repayment is reflected as a lien against the injured person's settlement proceeds.

One exception to the rule that workers compensation be repaid is where the worker's injury arises our of a motor vehicle accident. In that case, workers' compensation is paying the same benefits that no-fault insurance would ordinarily pay (lost earnings and medical expenses). Since no-fault benefits do not have to be repaid upon settlement, workers compensation benefits that are paid to worker for injuries sustained in a motor vehicle accident do not have to be repaid. In the event that workers' compensation paid out more benefits than no-fault would have given, there may be a lien, but the lien will be limited to the difference between what workers' compensation actually paid and what no-fault would have paid.

Liens may also be asserted by agencies that provide welfare benefits if the injured person has received such benefits associated with their injuries. Likewise, if the injured person has received benefits through their own private insurance, the private insurance company may also assert a lien on the settlement proceeds.

In some instances, the amount of the lien may be so high that it prevents a reasonable settlement from being reached. Under such circumstances, the attorney for the injured person may endeavor to negotiate a reduction of the lien. Lienholders frequently consent to such reductions, since they recognize that they may receive no money at all if the case proceeds to trial. By compromising, the lienholders will receive some money, which they may regard as a more attractive option than being faced with the risk of receiving no money at all.

ARE THERE TAXES ON SETTLEMENTS?

When you sustain a bodily injury, you often have medical bills, lost earnings, and pain and suffering. You would not have incurred any of these losses if your injury never occurred. Investment or business losses are often losses of money that the investor has saved over the course of many years. Discrimination cases often compensate the claimant for money that he or she could have earned, but for the discriminatory conduct.

Settlements and awards are intended to reimburse you for your losses; to make you whole again. You are not "ahead of the game" because of your case. For this reason, Congress has exempted most settlements and awards from tax. When you win your case, you probably will not pay taxes on the proceeds of your verdict or settlement.

SETTLEMENT CHECKLIST

You can only settle or win a case once. After your case has been settled or tried in court, you cannot go back and ask for more money, even if you find out that your damages are worse than you thought, or if new damages arise. Therefore, you should carefully consider the following:

1. What are the advantages of settling out of court?

2. Will I collect more or less if I go to court?

3. How long will I wait for my money if my case goes to court?

4. How much will I get after paying the lawyer?

5. When will I be paid?

6. Who will pay, and where does the money come from?

7. Are there additional parties against whom the claim should be asserted?

8. Are there any additional sources of settlement monies— for example, umbrella coverage, underinsurance coverage?

9. What benefits do I have in addition to my settlement (collateral sources)—for example, no-fault insurance, workers compensation, unemployment compensation, disability benefits?

10. Who pays for future medical bills?

11. Do I have to repay any liens or collateral sources?

12. Is there tax on the settlement amount?

13. What do my expert witnesses—for example, doctors, economists, accountants—say about my injuries?

14. What does my lawyer recommend?

15. If I am married, does my spouse have to agree to settle?

STATUTES OF LIMITATION

Statutes of limitations are time deadlines which are set by state law, and are applicable to virtually all legal claims. If you fail to bring a lawsuit on your claim within the appropriate statute of limitations, the claim will be barred forever, regardless of the seriousness of your injuries. Since statutes of limitations vary from state to state, and also differ based on the type of case that is being asserted, it is important to seek legal advice as soon as you are aware that you have been injured. By consulting with a lawyer, you will learn the applicable statute of limitations for your case.

The statute of limitations ordinarily begins to run on the date that an injury occurs, but certain conditions can extend the otherwise-applicable statute of limitations. Examples of events that might extend a statute of limitations include:

1. If an injury was not immediately susceptible to discovery—for example, if you underwent surgery and the doctor left a surgical instrument inside of you, you might not immediately discover that you had been injured. Your statute of limitations would probably begin to run from the date that you discovered that the implement had been left inside of you, not from the date of your surgery.

2. If the injured person was under the age of majority at the time that the injury occurred—for example, your child sustained a personal injury at age 11, and you elected to take no action with regard to pursuing a claim. The statute of limitations would be suspended (tolled) until your child reached the age of majority. Once your child reached the age of majority, he or she would be required to bring a claim on his or her own behalf within a specified amount of time.

3. If the injured person was not competent to bring action on his or her own behalf, the statute of limitations

would likewise be suspended or tolled during the period of disability.

Learning the correct statute of limitations that applies to your case is one of the most critical factors toward insuring recovery on your claim. Therefore, you should immediately seek legal counsel once you learn of your injury to clarify which statute of limitations applies.

CLAIMS AGAINST GOVERNMENT BODIES

Many cases involve claims against government bodies, whether at the federal, state or local level. Examples of such claims include:

1. If the government was the owner of a vehicle involved in an accident;

2. If an accident occurred on government property;

3. If a roadway maintained by a government body was defectively designed or maintained, thereby causing an accident.

If you believe that you have a claim against a government body, it is critical that you immediately seek legal advice. Virtually all government bodies require that injured persons notify the government body of the existence of their claim within a specified amount of time. This time limit is often very short, requiring filing within a matter of weeks after the incident giving rise to the claim. Failure to file such notification may prevent the injured person from ever recovering for their injuries.

This filing of a notice of the claim is separate from the requirement that a lawsuit be filed within the statute of limitations. As in all cases, lawsuits against government bodies must be filed within specific time deadlines. The timely filing of a notice of claim does not relieve the injured person of the obligation to start a lawsuit within the statute of limitations. Statutes of limitations against government bodies are also often shorter than statutes of limitations that apply to similar cases involving non-government defendants.

WORKERS'
COMPENSATION
CLAIMS

INTRODUCTION

If you are injured while you are on the job, Workers' Compensation will generally pay for your medical expenses and some portion of your lost wages. When you recover Workers' Compensation, you are not able to sue your employer. In some cases, however, you might sustain an injury on the job as a result of the conduct of somebody other than your employer. In such a case, even though you are entitled to collect Workers' Compensation, you might be able to bring an action against that other party. For example, if you were on the job using a machine that did not have proper safety devices, and you were hurt as a result, you could recover from Workers' Compensation **and** you could bring an action against the manufacturer and seller of the machine. Likewise, if you were driving a motor vehicle as part of your job, and you were involved in an accident and were injured, you could collect Workers' Compensation **and** you could sue the driver of the other vehicle. Cases such as these are called "third-party claims" because you are suing a third party other than your employer.

In such cases, Workers' Compensation will have what is called a lien on the proceeds that you receive from the third-party action. This means that Workers' Compensation will already have paid you for some of the same damages that you will recover from the third-party action (for example, lost wages and medical expenses). While you will repay Workers' Compensation for this lien, you can also receive additional money for the third-party action that you do not have to pay back.

THINGS TO DO IF YOU ARE HURT ON THE JOB

1. Seek medical attention. Advise your doctor of all your problems and that the accident occurred while at work. Follow your doctor's instructions for medical care.

2. Report the accident to your employer or supervisor and make sure that your employer takes a written report.

3. Get the name of your employer's workers compensation insurance carrier.

4. Obtain the names of all witnesses, along with their addresses and phone numbers.

5. Ask your doctor for a written statement of how long you should stay out of work.

6. If you were injured while using a piece of machinery, obtain the manufacturer's name, serial numbers, and any other information available about the machine. Take photographs of the machine, if possible.

7. Consult a personal injury lawyer to determine your legal rights with regard to claims for workers compensation and/or against any third party.

ABOUT THE AUTHOR

James J. Shapiro is a founder of the law firm of Shapiro & Shapiro, and is a member of the American Trial Lawyers Association and The Plaintiffs Securities Lawyers Group "PIABA." He graduated from the Boston University Law School Masters Program, is a member of the Florida, New York and Pennsylvania Bar Associations, and president of James J. Shapiro, P.A.

Mr. Shapiro started the law firm Shapiro & Shapiro with his father, Sidney Shapiro. James Shapiro has law offices in Dade and Broward Counties in Florida, as well as offices in Rochester, Syracuse and Buffalo, New York.

Mr. Shapiro has helped thousands of people by answering questions and telling the secrets used by insurance companies, corporations, and other defendants. He has been interviewed on radio talk shows across the country including the well-known program "Your Personal Finance," as well as on stations WEBT in New York City; WBVB and KDKA in Pittsburgh; WBZT in Palm Beach, Florida; WLIP in Kenosha, Wisconsin; KCED in San Diego/Carlsbad. As a result of Mr. Shapiro's frequent talk show broadcasts, listeners have created such a demand for his first book "INJURY VICTIMS RIGHTS TO MAXIMUM CASH" that over 20,000 copies are now in print.

James Shapiro is a tough, smart, aggressive lawyer who has made a lifetime commitment to helping victims win cash awards.

FREE UPDATES AND QUESTIONS:

If you have questions about this book . . .

If you would like free updates to this book . . .

If you would like to receive a free newsletter . . .

Contact **James Shapiro at 1-800-546-7777**

QUESTIONS

To receive the answers to your personal questions, please send your questions to the address below. We will attempt to answer your questions at no charge in our next newsletter or revised editions of this book.

To obtain free updates and newsletters, simply send your name and address to:

James Shapiro
Maximum Cash Book
1820 First Federal Plaza
Rochester, New York 14614

or phone 1–800–546–7777

NOTES